Iona – God's Energy

Iona – God's Energy

The Vision and Spirituality of the Iona Community

Norman Shanks

Hodder & Stoughton
LONDON SYDNEY AUCKLAND

First published in Great Britain 1999

10 9 8 7 6 5 4 3 2 1

British Library Cataloguing in Publication Data
A record for this book is available from the British Library

ISBN 0 340 72172 3

Typeset by Avon Dataset Ltd, Bidford-on-Avon, Warks

Printed and bound in Great Britain by
The Guernsey Press Co. Ltd, Channel Isles

Hodder & Stoughton Ltd
A Division of Hodder Headline PLC
338 Euston Road
London NW1 3BH

The author and publishers are grateful to the following for permission to quote:

Darton, Longman & Todd for an extract from *The Broken Body* by Jean Vanier (1988)

The Church in the Market Place Publications for extracts from *Vice Versa* by Jan Sutch Pickard (1997)

St Andrew Press for an extract from 'Pray Now', The Church of Scotland Panel on Worship (1998)

Edinburgh University Press for an extract from *Iona – The Earliest Poetry of a Celtic Monastery* by Thomas Owen Clancy and Gilbert Márkus (1995)

Canterbury Press, for extracts from *An Iona Prayer Book* by Peter Millar (1998)

WHERE IS IONA?

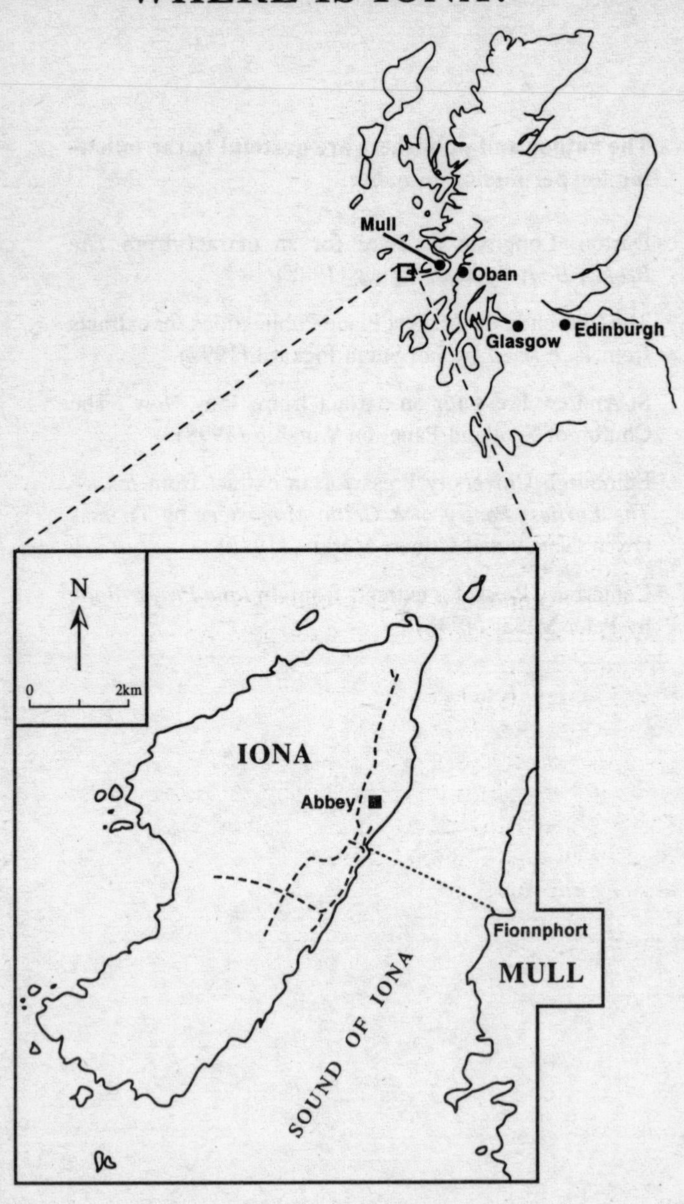

Contents

Preface

This book had its origins in an unexpected place! Invited to address the annual conference of the Scottish branch of the Movement for Christian Democracy in March 1997 – on social justice and the General Election prospects, as I recall – I was surprised to be asked by Annabel Robson, Commissioning Editor with Hodder and Stoughton, about the possibility of my writing a book about 'Iona spirituality'; and this is the result, although the gestation period, inevitably perhaps in view of the other demands on my time, has been rather longer than planned.

What follows is an exploration, and an opportunity to indulge in some personal reflection and ride some favourite hobby-horses. Inevitably it expresses and is influenced by my own spiritual journey over the years: indeed the task and process have helped me to see many things in a new light. It is not very systematic and certainly not conclusive (in any sense 'the last word') in its appraisal of the significance of the past and current activities and concerns of the Iona Community: for a more comprehensive account of the Community's story, Ron Ferguson's *Chasing the Wild Goose* (recently revised and published by the Community's Wild Goose Publications) is recommended. This is simply one person's viewpoint of the Community's vision, theology and understanding of spirituality, and the fact that I am currently Leader of the Community does not give what I say any extra authority or make it 'official policy', as Community Members would be quick to point out!

I wish to express my appreciation for the advice and encouragement I have received from many Members of the Community and some of the staff, especially at the Pearce Institute; it has been particularly helpful to have had access to the thinking and writing of others, and I acknowledge with gratitude the permissions readily granted to use and quote from material that has already been published elsewhere. My thanks are also due to Annabel Robson for her professional help and her tolerance with my failure to meet deadlines (boringly for the first time in my life!). I am immensely grateful to all those friends and family who have enhanced my own spiritual journey and influenced it for good over the years, and above all to Ruth, my wife, for her loving support over many years and in particular for her understanding during the last weeks as this book reached completion.

The royalties will go to the work of the Iona Community, which even with the tribulations of Leadership means more to me than I can express; and accordingly this book is dedicated to Community Members, Associates and staff, both past and present.

Norman Shanks
September 1998

1

What is Spirituality?

In their droves they come flocking off the ferry in the footsteps of Columba and Keats, Wordsworth, Mendelssohn and so many others, priests, politicians and 'punters' alike, 1200 of them a day now in high summer, day visitors, holiday-makers, guests at the Iona Community's islands centres. What is it that draws them to this little island of which Dr Johnson famously said, 'That man is not to be envied whose patriotism is not stirred on the plains of Marathon, whose piety is not warmed by the ruins of Iona'? Wherein does its fascination lie? Precisely what distinguishes it from other places of comparable significance in the history of Church and nation, just as naturally beautiful perhaps, and rather more peaceful for being off the tourists' beaten track? George MacLeod, founder of the modern Iona Community, described Iona as 'a thin place', with only, as it were, a tissue-paper separating the spiritual from the material. And many of those for whom Iona is special, and who go on from that to value also the work and concerns of the Iona Community, both on the mainland and on Iona itself, in trying to explain its appeal invariably at some point resort to the term which this book seeks to explore – 'spirituality'.

Visitors to Iona today see, in the centre of the cloisters in the restored Benedictine Abbey, a striking statue cast out of bronze. Some people see its strange shape as a bomb; and indeed it has been used effectively many times over the years, whether in worship or discussion, as a focus for reflection on the Christian's vocation to peace-making or on the Iona Community's opposition to nuclear weapons. For others it is like a bulb, speaking of growth, new life, resurrection. The truth is that, just as evocatively and dramatically, the statue depicts the Incarnation. It is called 'The Descent of the Spirit', and its story is told in Ron Ferguson's book about the history of the Iona Community, *Chasing the Wild Goose.* It is the work of an American Jew called Jacob Lipchitz, bears a French inscription ('Jacob Lipchitz, Jew, faithful to the religion of his ancestors, has made this Virgin for the better understanding of human beings on this earth so that the Spirit may prevail') and is one of a set of three statues commissioned by an American woman: there is an identical work in the United States in the 'Roofless Church', a community experiment at New Harmony, Indiana, and another, the original 'Notre Dame de Liesse', in a Roman Catholic (Dominican) church at Assy in central France. The dove descending, large-eyed, all-seeing, the figure of the Virgin in the centre, within the heart-shaped canopy, womb-like too, representing humanity, open, receptive, but blind, the lamb below – also blind – the three supportive angelic figures, unseeing too, all combine to create an unfathomable dynamic of energy and mystery.

The statue stands in the middle of what was for the medieval monks the place of the common life, around which the daily life of the modern Abbey ebbs and flows relentlessly. The spirit is thus represented truly at the centre of human life. Here at the heart of its island home is summed up visually, symbolically, how the Iona Community understands and expresses spirituality. Despite its dramatic, apparently unconventional appearance, in one sense the statue is very traditional, suggesting an orthodoxy, even a conservatism in its interpretation of Scripture. The Jewish origins of the sculptor hint, however, at something more challenging, crossing boundaries, exploring unfamiliar territory, reaching into unknown, deep places. All this too is true to and consistent with how the Iona Community sees its commitment to the 'rediscovery of spirituality', on the one hand rooted in the historic Christian faith, on the other open to new possibilities, seeking to discover and embody relevance to the needs and situations of our contemporary world.

Those who hope to find in this book a conclusive definition of spirituality, even the last word on the Iona Community's approach to spirituality, may well be disappointed. Spirituality cannot be pinned down so easily. George MacLeod once described the birth of Jesus Christ as 'an inherent explosion into matter, setting up a chain reaction of igniting love'; and in that statement there are not only pointers to the general understanding of spirituality that still permeates the Community's concerns and priorities but also the clear indication of the potentially shattering, life-changing implications of the Christian Gospel. Perhaps those who see the Lipchitz statue as a bomb are more accurate than they realise!

Spirituality is very much in vogue these days, almost something of a growth industry: the interest in personal development is in a sense the semi-respectable face of the prevailing individualistic, rather introverted ethos of our times. There is a rich vein to be tapped by those who set themselves up as quasi-consultants, professing expertise in this field! In the bookshops, in North America and Australia as well as Britain, a remarkable amount of shelf-space is devoted to this area, often described as 'personal inspiration', 'self-help', 'body and soul', or the like. Workshops, courses, and conferences on Celtic spirituality in particular prove immensely popular. The next chapter will explore the contemporary context rather more fully. But it is clear that one of the factors that impels people towards Iona, interests them in the work of the Iona Community and movements and groups that share some of the Community's concerns is the search for meaning, value and depth in life. The outpouring of emotion evident on a huge scale at the time of the death and funeral of Princess Diana was an expression of this phenomenon. In Britain today, as in many other parts of the so-called 'developed' world, there is widespread disillusionment with the prevailing market-driven culture of acquisitive individualism, and a need, both personal and communal, that may be recognised only infrequently, for purpose and belonging. Ultimately, this is an issue about spirituality, and, even if it is seldom described as such, it is a religious matter. People are looking for God, or, perhaps more accurately, responding to God's reaching out to them, God's prompting within them. The missionary challenge facing the churches today is that, whether on account of prejudice, ignorance or previous adverse experience, much of this searching does not look to traditional religion or the institutional Church. And yet the Christian Gospel is 'good news' precisely because it promises hope for all. Its message is that God's love embraces every human situation, that no individual is beyond the scope of God's grace, that in Jesus Christ is embodied this reality that all things are made new, and that God's kingdom, in all its fullness, is already breaking into our frail, flawed world.

For its part, as we shall see more fully later on, the Community has, since its creation, been committed to finding 'new ways to touch the hearts of all', as it is put in one of the Community's favourite prayers, said whenever Members gather together in local groups or plenary meetings, and repeated regularly also on Iona in the service each Friday morning. In so doing it is deliberately, and in a variety of ways, attempting to address this issue of contemporary spirituality, playing a part in helping those who recognise within themselves an emptiness, a hunger and thirst for substance and a sense of significance. There is no question of the Community believing that it has all the answers or is in any sense alone in seeking to respond to these deeply felt needs. Far from it: what we do we do alongside and in solidarity with all others who are inspired by and committed to the vision and values of the kingdom, and in dependence on the grace of God. What is distinctive about the Community, however, what seems to appeal to all those who are attracted and interested by its work, are certain features that together are fundamental to the Community's understanding of its approach to spirituality, namely, the significance of worship, both underpinning and overarching all else; a commitment to ecumenism, inclusive, transcending all traditional church divisions; and the integration of spiritual and social concerns, reflecting the 'wholeness' of life, the universal relevance of the Gospel, the linking of personal religious obedience and action for social and political change.

In the late 1980s the Community embarked on an exercise that may have been a little pretentious: we drew up a strategic plan! The primary object was to identify working priorities for the next five years or so. After a process of extended consultation and discussion the plan was completed and approved, and it included several agreed 'areas of concern'. One of these, to which the Community remains committed, is described as the 'rediscovery of spirituality'.

Spirituality, as is already obvious, is a tantalisingly elusive and slippery term. It is much easier to illustrate than to define. There may be a tendency to assume that the pursuit of a deeper, fuller spirituality is self-evidently 'a good thing'. But this is far from true: spirituality itself is a morally neutral concept; so there are good and bad, well-founded and misguided, healthy and damaging approaches to spirituality. For its part the Iona Community would want to distance itself from any understanding of spirituality that is not rooted and grounded in the realities and experience of life. There have been suggestions that the Iona Community has embraced some of the esoteric, ethereal, non-Christian features of New Age thinking. It is hard to see how anyone with direct knowledge or first-hand experience of the Community's work, either on Iona or on the mainland, can be so mistaken. On the contrary, while the attempts to explore and develop new, more relevant and participative ways to worship may be unfamiliar to some, while the inclusion of dance, drama or other creative approaches in programmes and events may appear challenging, the underlying thinking and theology have sometimes been criticised as disappointingly orthodox; much less out of the ordinary than had been expected or even hoped for! And it must be remembered, in any case, that New Age thinking is itself highly eclectic and contains strands that are perfectly compatible and consistent with mainstream Christianity.

The truth is that spirituality is not something that is abstract or detached from the everyday realities of life, the range of human situations and experiences to which it is related. Spirituality is essentially contextual, as indeed is the whole discipline of theology. Nothing can be seen or fully understood apart from the context out of which it emerges, which inevitably shapes and influences it. The insights may have a degree of timeless significance, elements of the process may be universally instructive, but they are also products of particular experience and it should not be assumed that they can be transferred elsewhere or applied to another person and situation without a measure of critical reflection and adaptation.

My impression is that until relatively recently the word 'spirituality' would not have figured prominently in the thinking or conversation of Iona Community Members; there is little evidence of its use in any of the books or papers which date from the Community's early years. And in this, in a sense, the Community simply reflects the spirit and culture of the times, both then and now. Nonetheless, down the years the life of the Community, and the stories of its Members, demonstrate a consistency of purpose in living out the faith, an integration of prayer and politics, of work and worship, a refusal to compartmentalise life into, for example, separate 'spiritual' and 'secular' aspects, on the grounds, as George MacLeod put it so memorably, that God's Spirit permeates 'every blessed thing'.

When some years ago the Community identified the 'rediscovery of spirituality' as a priority of concern, such interest was generated that a special 'fringe' meeting, arranged outside the formal programme during Community Week on Iona when Members gather each year, attracted a surprisingly large number of people. From the discussion it was clear not only that there was an intense interest in exploring different Members' understanding of spirituality and the possibility of coming to some 'common mind', but also that there was much concern lest current fashions, and in particular New Age thinking, should divert attention away from what many held to be the Community's basic perspective. That approach is perhaps summed up in one of George MacLeod's favourite stories – recounted without attribution or acknowledgement by the Archbishop of Canterbury in his 1997 Christmas message, broadcast throughout Asda superstores in England and widely reported in the media! The story is about a stained-glass window in an inner-city church with the inscription of the angels' hymn 'Glory to God in the highest'. A vandal's stone had removed one of the panes of glass, so that now the message read 'Glory to God in the High St'! That speaks of a rooted, engaged spirituality with which, for all their diversity, the entire membership of the Iona Community would identify, so basic is it to our belonging together and to our common purpose.

One of the Community Members, Kathy Galloway, theologian, author and poet, has described spirituality as 'that which ultimately moves you – the fundamental motivation of your life', or, to put it slightly differently, how we live out what we most profoundly believe. Another Community Member, in the course of a consultation on spirituality that was carried out several years ago, described it as 'living life to the full – having an abundant life in a true sense which is free from guilt and open to other people'. Yet another Member, Ruth Harvey, is director of the Council of Churches for Britain and Ireland's Ecumenical Spirituality Project. This project, according to its own description, 'works alongside all who have faith in Christ, who seek God by living from the inside out, and are pioneering new ways of living in the faith', and offers resources for 'those seeking to explore an integrated spirituality for today' – 'not as an alternative to their "church" identity . . . but as a rediscovery of how to *be* church'. Recently, under the auspices of this project, there have been special consultations, described as 'conversations', relating to 'spirituality in the city' and spirituality with regard to justice and peace issues, providing opportunities for reflection on experience and sharing stories in 'the belief that learning is most powerful when we are enabled to see ourselves as our own resource, when we are empowered to recognise the Holy Spirit at work within our own lives and so to see the wisdom of our own words and thoughts'.

In a booklet produced by Ruth Harvey's predecessors as directors of the project, Joan Puls and Gwen Cashmore, they explain the approach further: 'ecumenical spirituality is discipleship, with its global implications, lived locally. It is the steady commitment to earth faith in a particular place and to be open to connections with the world Church. Its hallmarks are – hospitality, vulnerability, inclusiveness.' They go on to say, 'Spirituality is not the "possession" of any one group or tradition. It is the journey, undertaken in every age, to incarnate the gospel and to express the deepest human longings, beliefs and values.'

A similar general approach, thoroughly rooted yet inclusive and expansive, is to be found at an early stage in the work of the Community's working group, when Peter Millar, then recently returned from twelve years' work in India, later (1995 to 1998) Warden of Iona Abbey, touched a chord of approval with many Community Members when he quoted the American peace activist and writer, Jim Forest, who in the preface to a book about religious life in Russia and experience of spirituality there referred to the concept of 'Dukhovnost'. This means literally 'quality of spirit . . . While referring to the intimate life of prayer, it also suggests moral capacity, courage, wisdom, mercy, social responsibility, a readiness to forgive, a way of life centred on love . . . in short all that happens in your life when God is the central point of reference.' And again, from a recent study by the World Council of Churches, taking the exploration of the multi-faceted character of spirituality into different areas, 'Spirituality is the exercise by which people reach beyond themselves on what Max Weber calls "life forces" of existence. Spirituality is story, memory, symbols, language, poetry and song. Spirituality is the capacity for resistance and the courage to construct new alternatives and paradigms. Spirituality is the energy that transforms relationships.'

These illustrations and examples, from the life of the Community and some of its wider contacts, are offered as pointers rather than definitions; what they have in common is a striking dynamic quality, having to do fundamentally with the development and exploration of our human identity, and above all the strong characteristic that they are related to and grounded in action. This is a perspective reflected also in the description of spirituality by Jon Sobrino, Latin American liberation theologian, as 'doing things with spirit', or in the remarks of George MacLeod (one of the Community's founder's apparently few comments on the subject) – 'The true mark of Christian spirituality is to get one's teeth into things. Painstaking service to (hu)mankind's most material needs is the essence of spirituality.' In a sense this may still be taken to stand as the heart and ground of the Community's approach. It has excellent scriptural authority, (for example, in the familiar parable of the Last Judgment in Matthew 25, where it was those who cared for the needy who found acceptance with God; in the words attributed to Jesus in Matthew 7:21: 'Not everyone who says to me, "Lord, Lord" will enter the kingdom of heaven, but only those who do the will of my heavenly Father;' and through the insight in James 2:17, dismissed by Martin Luther as an 'epistle of straw' but important nonetheless within the Christian tradition: 'So with faith; if it does not lead to action it is a lifeless thing.')

John Harvey, previously (1988–95) Leader of the Community, is one of a number of Iona Community Members who lead workshops and speak at events about spirituality themes. Since completing his term as Leader he has worked with the Craighead Institute of Faith and Life, an ecumenical Christian project based in Glasgow, whose approach is rooted in Ignatian spirituality, with its fundamental principle that God can be discovered in all things and an emphasis on personal discernment and the significance of committed discipleship, lived out in the midst of everyday life. This standpoint is reflected also in Gerard Hughes' recent book, *God, Where Are You?*, based on his work over recent years in exploring and promoting a spirituality appropriate to the vocation of people involved in justice and peace work, in the course of which he discovered that those so involved

> tended to develop spirituality more quickly and more deeply than those who were not [because] God is the God of justice and peace and it was in the doing of these things that these people were meeting God. Because of the difficulties, frustrations and opposition they met with . . .

> they experienced depths of pain unknown to them before. In their pain they became more aware of their own fragility and of their need for prayer.

As we shall see later this insight is reflected also within the Community's experience down the years.

Although within the Reformed tradition there may have been a tendency to regard a concern for spirituality almost as alien to mainstream orthodoxy, as in some other aspects of church life (for example, liturgy and church governance), this owes much to subsequent deliberate attempts to develop distinctive patterns that could not be identified with Roman Catholic influences or approaches. Moreover, according to the evidence of the writings of Luther and Calvin, it is hardly in line with the practice and intentions of the Reformers themselves. More recently there are signs of a readiness within the Reformed tradition to adopt a more eclectic and inclusive approach and to express more accurately something of the original Reformation spirit in this area. At the meeting of the General Council of the World Alliance of Reformed Churches, held at Debrecen, Hungary, in August 1997, on the theme 'Breaking the chains of injustice', the preparatory study material contained a significant passage exploring the shared heritage of those within the Reformed tradition. This had a clear emphasis on *spiritual* formation of community: 'the sixteenth century reformers . . . wanted the Christian life to be lived out by all Christians in their many vocations. This understanding of spirituality shapes and enriches the worship life of Reformed communities.' Here is interesting confirmation of the significance accorded, within the beginnings of the Reformed tradition, to the place of the sacraments, Scripture and preaching in relation to spirituality, so often subsequently dismissed as an alien pursuit, but increasingly and thankfully now recovered as a thoroughly appropriate and indeed central interest for all who seek to explore and deepen their faith. And the strong links between spirituality and worship affirmed by the Iona Community place it clearly within the mainstream of this tradition, within which there are now clear signs of an eagerness for a wider sharing and an opening out to embrace more inclusively other insights and people within the broader Christian family.

At present Celtic spirituality in particular attracts intense interest. It is perhaps significant that individual dissatisfaction with the prevailing culture of acquisitive individualism and the pressures and tensions of modern urban life are driving people to seek personal tranquillity elsewhere, often in remote and beautiful places in Ireland, Scotland and Wales, and to explore the past as a possible source of ideas for ordering things better. So, over recent years, we have found that considerable media attention has focused on Iona and Celtic spirituality, and within the Iona Community we get enquiries by letter, phone call and e-mail (very often emanating from across the Atlantic!) day after day in our Glasgow office and on Iona, and this too is what brings many people to Iona and interests them in the Community generally. But so much of what is purveyed and perceived as 'Celtic spirituality' is misguided or at least incomplete. David Lodge's novel *Therapy*, which is very much a product of our times in its exploration of themes of therapy, religion and relationship in and out of marriage, and its setting for the most part in the world of television, very strikingly makes the point, against the background of pilgrimage, that healing and fulfilment are ultimately to be found not in continual navel-gazing but in self-giving relationships, by turning outwards to the real world. The idea of pilgrimage, a journey of faith prompted by or seeking a fuller understanding of God, is central to spirituality, particularly within the Celtic tradition; but there is an important distinction between the journey that is essentially about getting away from something, somewhere or someone, and that which is undertaken with a purpose.

The medieval discipline of *peregrinatio* was the outward expression of a journey that involved inner change, a symbol of the journey towards deeper faith and greater holiness, towards God, that is the Christian life.

So much of the contemporary pursuit of Celtic spirituality is escapist, romantic, nostalgic, individualistic and self-indulgent, a flight to the edge, a quest for remote, beautiful, tranquil places, redolent of a golden past, getting away from the pressures, tensions and incessant demands of life's hurly-burly. But a close study of the Celtic tradition (see, for example, *The Celtic Way* by Ian Bradley, and *A World Made Whole* by Esther de Waal) reveals that Celtic spirituality was not about escape but above all about engagement – with the humdrum particularities and practicalities of life (like digging the garden, milking the cow), with the reality of nature, so much more savage, dark and exacting than modern sanitised, idealised attitudes would often suggest. This was based on a perpetual sense of the presence of God, on the view that God is to be encountered not only in the beauty and peace of nature in isolated places, but also in the immediate, in the rough-and-tumble, in the very middle of life. As Joan Puls and Gwen Cashmore, formerly of the CCBI's Ecumenical Spirituality Project say, 'The Celt was very much a God-intoxicated person whose life was embraced on all sides by the Divine Being, the Trinity. But this presence was always mediated through the finite, this-world reality, so that it would be difficult to imagine a spirituality more down to earth.'

Thus authentic spirituality, reflecting the insights of the Celtic tradition, stresses the communal aspect, the importance of the Celtic monastic communities as centres of hospitality and healing, the significance of social interaction, affirming that God is to be discovered and experienced in the complex dynamic of human relationships as well as in solitary meditation. Approached thus spirituality is to be seen as thoroughly world-affirming, integrating the different aspects of our lives;

it is about various kinds of *connectedness*, all of which are themselves interrelated. First of all there is our inner connectedness, being 'all-together' within ourselves. This may be more an aspiration than a reality for most of us: we explore later (in Chapter 5) how the Community's concern for and understanding of healing relates to its approach to spirituality. The communal prayer of confession used in the daily morning service in Iona Abbey, and also whenever Community Members gather to worship elsewhere, acknowledges 'that our lives and the life of our world are broken by our sin'. Our spiritual development is a journey towards becoming whole people, a process of growth which involves increasing self-understanding, becoming integrated personalities, aware of but more or less comfortable with our strengths and weaknesses.

The second aspect is our connectedness in relationship with one another. We are 'bound up in the bundle of life' with other people, as Reinhold Niebuhr's famous prayer puts it; it is not possible to separate our personal fulfilment from how we look at and deal with others; the realisation of our individual identity is to be found within the context of relationships. Our well-being is dependent on the well-being of others; and correspondingly we are diminished by the suffering of others. Only when we are in right relationship with other people, is there the possibility of being 'all right' within, at ease with ourselves. This is the eternal truth that lies behind the New Testament commandments, which of course are inextricably interlinked, mutually dependent almost – to love God and our neighbour as ourselves. But even more than that, perhaps; there is another gospel insight which takes this farther still. We gain life through being ready to give life away – so hard, so challenging; but for most of us there are likely to have been fleeting glimpses and experiences of this reality within our own lives. The problem is that the adoption of such a mode of living as standard runs counter to our very strong natural inclination to pursue our own self-interest as the basic priority.

Nonetheless this is our calling; and it is only by being truly *connected* with others in the orientation of our lives that we shall achieve the inner connectedness, the self-fulfilment and along with it the connectedness with God that is our spiritual goal, both our destiny and the deepest desire of our inmost hearts. Thus the third aspect of our connectedness, binding it all together, energising our relatedness with others, is our connectedness with God, not separately from the other aspects but somehow interpenetrating and undergirding all else. The chapters on worship and the development of personal spirituality explore this more fully, but already the central significance of the Eucharist becomes evident, since through it at once in both symbol and immediate experience we come closer to God and closer to one another.

I am not sure when or where it suddenly occurred to me, as an aid to exploring and reflecting on these themes of spirituality, how helpful and multi-dimensional the word 'abandon' was. As a verb it carries obvious connotations of giving up and laying down, the denial of self for the sake of pursuing others' interests. But as a noun it suggests not only self-forgetfulness but also joy and fulfilment; and the central syllable has a thoroughly communal ring! The sense of energy and depth to be found in reflecting on 'abandon' link in once more with the understanding of spirituality as having to do with connectedness. The fullness of life that is at one and the same time the longing of every human heart and God's promise and purpose for each one of us depends on all these aspects of connectedness being bound up together, reflecting an integrated life. Our inner connectedness, our connectedness with one another, our connectedness with God are inextricably interlinked. As two others of the anonymous contributions to the Community's previously mentioned consultation put it, 'A true spirituality is completely interwoven with a life of loving service to others;' and

> I suppose George MacLeod is one of my gurus, and he always says: 'Christ was not crucified on a cathedral altar between two candlesticks, but on a city rubbish dump between two thieves.' That witness is attractive, magnetic even. We need to make it. We need to deny the false image of individualistic pietism, which the word 'spirituality' engenders. Spirituality has a missionary urgency.

One of the Community Members, in the course of the same exercise, referred to the friendship of his grand-uncle, a parish minister in the Western Isles for many years, with Alexander Carmichael, collector of *Carmina Gadelica*, source of so much Celtic material:

> They talked and studied and the grand-uncle always said that he voted for *Biblical* spirituality. We believe the Bible teaches us that the material world is not an obstacle to spirituality but a gift of God, the area of our obedience. Biblical spirituality is not a renunciation of the material but an insistence upon its right and Godly use. Social justice is an authentic expression of this. It is the story right through the years of the community of keeping a balance, a wholeness, a total faith.

Drawing all this together one gets a sense of the depth, the scope, the dynamic of spirituality, that nothing is to be excluded from the workings of the Spirit: not only prayer, but also politics, social justice, personal relationships become the concern of that living, moving presence. And one gains a glimpse, however fleeting, of the boundless horizons, the multi-dimensional complexity, the range of themes involved in interpreting and approaching spirituality in terms of an energising kind of connectedness, promising fulfilment, insistently demanding, providing challenging pointers towards discernment, imagination, risk, dreaming, exploring – pushing the boat out. This is well summed up by Kenneth Leech, Anglican community theologian in inner London, who, although coming with his Anglo-Catholic background from a rather different perspective, nonetheless has much in common with the views and approach of the Iona Community. He offers many helpful insights in this area, especially in his two most recent books, *The Eye of the Storm* and *The Sky is Red*: 'Spirituality is not a sub-division of Christian discipleship. It is the root, the source, the life. The Spirit gives life and nourishes the whole. Spirituality is a corporate discipline, a corporate experience.'

We bless you, our God,
mighty sovereign power,
gentle caring mother.
You do not forget your children.
We bless you, our God,
For your great gifts to us:
creation – fragile and fascinating,
Scripture – revealing your truth.
And you bless us . . .
with your forgiving love,
with the vision of your kingdom,
shedding light in our darkness.
Bless us and disturb us
with that vision of your kingdom,
and as we voice our hopes to you now,
  may they strengthen us,
  reassure us
  and move us . . .
Into the mess of this world a fragile child will come –
yelling in the night for his mother,
needing milk and clean linen . . .
We pin our hopes on you, little baby,

Our God – pushed out into the world,
through pain and into poverty.
Our God is with us and our hope is reborn.
AMEN.
(Wild Goose Resource Group, *Cloth for the Cradle*)

2

The Contemporary Context

The highest point on Iona is only about 300 feet above sea level – Dun-I, meaning the hill-fort of the island. But it is a place where many people have had 'mountain-top experiences', not just because of the magnificent views on a clear day – the pink rocks of Mull and the mass of Ben More to the east; the Paps of Jura away to the south; to the west Coll and Tiree, the ancient cornfield of the monks; and in the north, beyond Staffa and the string of the Treshnish islands, the hills of Rhum, and, if you are really lucky, the Cuillins of Skye. Mountain-top experiences are not just about views. They are about a different way of seeing things: this is what happens on Dun-I and on many other mountain-tops too. The experience, not necessarily on its own but cumulatively and in the context of all sorts of other things that are happening in our lives, changes the shape of our perceptions, and may even change our sense of priorities.

Even in the depths of winter the ferry, running on a much less frequent service, carries visitors to Iona. They are not deterred by the increased possibility of being storm-bound or by the knowledge that almost everything is closed out of season. The attraction is deep and compelling, much more than sheer curiosity value or another guide-book recommendation to be ticked off. And in the winter there may be more of a chance to appreciate the true spirit of the place – to understand the context more fully than is possible among the hordes of tourists in high summer. The tantalising questions keep coming back: is Iona really different from similar Hebridean islands with their own tranquil beauty and white beaches? Is it all really so mysterious and intangible? Does it have to do with more than the unique blend of historical and religious significance and the rich personal memories of people and experiences that each visitor takes away?

It is perhaps understandable that so many who come to Iona assume that the Iona Community is to be found on Iona and are surprised to discover that this is not so; the concept of a dispersed community may at first be a little hard to grasp. But too often the existence of a community of local people on Iona is overlooked – they, after all, are the 'real' Iona community, the population of around 100 men, women and children whose lives go on alongside all the comings and goings. They are an important part of the landscape and life of Iona, of the context to which the work of the Iona Community must relate and within which it must be understood. And in the same sort of way any attempt to explore approaches to spirituality, whether of the Iona Community or anyone else, must take account of the contemporary context.

The conventional analysis tends to conclude that contemporary British society is characterised by pluralism and secularism, postmodern in its reaction against authority and institutions. It has to be said, of course, that even viewed from a Christian standpoint this is not necessarily regrettable – not all bad! After all, authorities and institutions may become tired and out of touch with the needs and demands of changing times; those who carry responsibility within them may develop policies and pursue priorities that are misguided and do not lead in the best direction: so the authorities and institutions must be challenged and questioned. And pluralism is not necessarily a bad thing, for uniformity may be stultifying and diversity enriching; and while it may be tempting to disparage and dismiss the 'pick-and-mix' character of modern society, within which there is seen by some to exist a *laisser-faire* approach within which anything goes, or a kind of supermarket of ideas, all of equal validity, this is by no means the only possible Christian response.

Alternatively the position is both intellectually respectable and practically sustainable that on the one hand recognises the value of an open-ended process of dialogue and exploration, acknowledging the mutual benefits to be gained through the sharing of insights and the limitations of all attempts to understand the ultimate and express the inexpressible, and on the other hand sees the need to draw the line against what may be morally or conceptually unacceptable and to witness to personal conviction in a way that does not judge, threaten or seek to browbeat into agreement. Equally, secularism is not to be equated with Godlessness; on the contrary it may open up new ways of discerning, discovering, experiencing and encountering God – more creatively and flexibly, released from what may often have become an ecclesiastical straitjacket, the temptation to regard God and the things of God as an exclusive preserve and possession, the cramped and clamping shackles of formal religion that too frequently seeks to pin God down, keep God conveniently 'in a box'.

So the challenges that postmodernism brings are thoroughly to be welcomed. But over and against that, one of the less positive characteristics of postmodernism is the disintegration of the sense of communal values. The philosopher Alasdair MacIntyre exploring this in *After Virtue* and also in *Whose Justice, Which Rationality?*, describes our times as 'the new dark ages, where there is no shared understanding of the nature of virtue, the content of justice, or the definition of evil', and he calls for the rediscovery of virtue and community; he maintains that 'moral consensus cannot be sustained except in the foundation of some kind of agreement about fundamental beliefs'. The problem today, of course, is the absence of precisely this kind of agreement, the recognition and acceptance of an objective authority or meta-narrative that overarches and undergirds all human activity and concerns.

Michael Ignatieff, writing in the magazine *Prospect* in March 1997, referred to the complex and fragmented moral context:

> In belief systems we are no longer of one faith; in our private lives, we are no longer within one family model; in the nation itself, no longer under the stable or uncontested domination of the English; and we no longer belong to a community of common origins. We are living in what Isaiah Berlin called a 'pluralist world of incommensurable and sometimes incompatible visions of the good'. (Quoted by Alf Young in *The Herald,* 27 March 1997)

Chief Rabbi Jonathan Sacks, in his 1990 Reith Lectures on *The Persistence of Faith* described this as 'the crumbling of the moral ecology'. He said,

> The values that once led us to regard one as intrinsically better than another – and which gave such weight to words like good and bad – have disintegrated, along with the communities and religious traditions in which we learned them. Now we choose because we choose. Because it is what we want; or it works for us; or it feels right to me. Once we have dismantled a world in which larger values held sway, what is left are success and self-expression, the key-values of an individualistic culture.

But there is a paradox here, of course. While there are clearly parts of the analysis of MacIntyre and Sacks that are almost beyond dispute, and which present a huge contemporary missionary challenge to the churches (which we go into a little more fully in Chapter 11), nonetheless the Iona Community's experience, both at our islands centres and elsewhere, points also in the opposite direction. To an extent we live in a post-Christian society, or perhaps more correctly a post-church society, characterised by what has been called, because people's minds and attitudes are so much less God-centred than previously, 'the secularisation of the consciousness' or, because of the reduced influence of the Church within the life of society and the emergence of new patterns of believing and belonging, 'the de-institutional-isation of religion'. Nonetheless it remains true that, as has already been said, there are many people who are interested, even desperate, to pursue their quest for belonging, for spirituality and social concern, the search for meaning, depth, value, connectedness; but they tend to do so outside the life of the Church.

The political commentators have been making the same kind of points. Writing in the spring of 1997, and attempting to set out an 'agenda for the new era' before the forthcoming General Election, Will Hutton, Editor of *The Observer*, said,

> The difficulties with individualist, laisser-faire capitalism are manifest. In the first place markets throw up a distribution of income and of risk that challenge any conception of fairness or justice. It may be possible to justify very high salaries for genuine enterprise at the top while simultaneously deploring the forces that are driving real wages down at the bottom because both are rational in economic terms, but for how long can we consider the distribution of risk and opportunity that accompany such incomes as congruent with any concept of a just society? Once we lose the integrative cement of shared values and of the belief that everyone has some claim on the whole, we are lost; it is the road to a new barbarism.

We live now in an age where not only church-going appears to be in decline, but even where, within the life and liturgy of the churches, the sermon holds much less significance than previously – whether because of people's shorter attention span in an age accustomed to communication through headlines, sound-bites and tele-adverts, or the shift in cultural and educational patterns with doubts about the effectiveness of the lecturing mode and more emphasis on an experiential approach to learning, or the social changes whereby the minister is no longer one of the few educated founts of wisdom within the local community, or whatever. And now it tends to be political columnists and social commentators to whom we look for the prophetic analysis and the challenging word, very often expressed through a profound concern, readily perceived and understood as deeply spiritual, for social values and priorities.

One of my own favourites in this respect is the Scottish writer and broadcaster, Joyce McMillan, who consistently, and frequently like a voice crying in the wilderness, decries what she has described as 'the militant what-I-have-I-hold materialism' and calls, not least from those with decision-making responsibilities in society, for a recovery of civic virtues 'like justice, truthfulness, stability, generosity, perseverance, mercy, humility, and magnanimity, which simply means 'greatness of spirit' '. So, redolent of the choice between life and death with which Moses, at the end of his life, presented the people of Israel on the threshold of their entry to the promised land, we in our own time are presented on the one hand with the road to a new barbarism, the selfish individualism that subordinates social responsibility to personal prosperity, and on the other with a sense of and commitment to the common good of the kind that has inspired and influenced the churches' relationship with society for many years.

Within the current political context there are many who would argue that social justice is scarcely any more acceptable a concept or objective than socialism itself! Only a couple of years ago I had the sobering experience of being accused by one of Scotland's most left-wing Members of the European Parliament, a man with the reputation of being virtually an unreconstructed Marxist, of engaging in sound-bites when at a public discussion I referred to social justice. Doubted by the far left, honoured in theory by New Labour (although a fuller judgment must await the outcome of the package of economic, welfare and social policy measures that is constrained by the commitment to maintain Conservative public spending limits for the first two years of government), social justice has long been dismissed as a mirage by the ideologues and gurus of the New Right – on the basis that it is impossible to secure any consensus as to the principles of social justice (the postmodern argument again); and in any case they argue that for injustice to exist there must have been intentional coercion – it cannot just happen through a concatenation of social and personal causes and events.

At an Iona Community plenary meeting in February 1998, the Secretary of State for Scotland, a long-standing friend of a number of Community Members, accepted an invitation to share his reflections on the political situation after almost a year in office. And issues relating to social justice inevitably featured prominently in the subsequent discussion. Since its inception the Community has regarded the pursuit of social justice as a priority, inseparably part of its approach to and understanding of spirituality. There is so much in modern society that is out of line with the vision and values of the kingdom of God which motivated the attacks of the Old Testament prophets on the moral shortcomings of their own times. It is a strong and inspiring New Testament theme not least in the teaching of Jesus, and has inspired social reformers and dissident radicals down the centuries. This is the mainspring of the political commitment that is discussed more fully in Chapter 9. The evidence of social and physical deprivation, with the well-established links with the kind of spiritual, moral and emotional disintegration so often associated with poverty, unemployment, inadequate community facilities, poor health, sub-standard housing, and low educational attainment, is an offence within any society that claims to be civilised and caring. The motivation towards action for change inevitably has both spiritual and political roots, springing from Gospel imperatives, solidarity with the marginalised, concern wherever intrinsic human worth is violated, dissatisfaction with injustice and exploitation, and much else besides. But the pursuit of such an agenda, with its clear communal perspective, is to a large extent counter-cultural, swimming against the tide of popular trends and majority preferences.

The prevailing ethos of our times is a self-indulgent kind of possessive individualism that has insidiously wormed its way into the lives and consciousness of us all. Melanie Phillips, formerly of *The Observer*, has memorably and pithily described this as 'the beggar-my-neighbour morality of egotistical self-realisation'! As a leader in the same newspaper put it prior to the 1997 General Election, 'The enterprise culture of responsibility, risk and reward has given way to the lottery culture of random selection and rampant greed.' Some sociologists attempt to explain this in terms of a deterministic neo-Darwinism – a process of natural selection and survival of the fittest; and while such an analysis may have some appeal for those who wish to see individuals as passive victims of circumstances and those who wish to stress the influence of nurture and environment, it is clearly unsatisfactory for leaving no room for the exercise of personal moral choice or for apparently ruling out the possibility of outside intervention, whether by the state or other agency, to provide beneficial facilities or bring about improvement.

So it comes about that people's identities and status tend to be determined by what they have rather than who (or what) they are; getting on is regarded as more important than getting on with other people and caring for them. The question Jesus was asked – 'Who is my neighbour?' – assumes a different significance in a mobile, fragmented society where so many people, shut up in their own little boxes and tense, so busy lives, wondering where the next short-term contract will be coming from, do not know who lives next door or across the road. Within our well-fabricated cocoons sustained by all the latest high-tech state-of-the-art gadgetry, we have the illusion of independence. To take this farther and to explore the dehumanising effect and spiritual significance of this situation, it is perhaps salutary and instructive to reflect on two contemporary symbols that somehow epitomise the spirit and priorities of our times. On the one hand there is the personal stereo, reflecting the electronic isolation of so many people's lives, locked into a private world of thumping repetitiveness, at once apparently cut off from interpersonal communication and yet paradoxically at the same time often intruding infuriatingly into other people's space. The other symbol is the National Lottery whose features and popularity demonstrate so clearly the spiritual depths to which our nation has sunk, reflecting the abandonment of the sense of communal responsibility that requires worthwhile social projects to be funded as a matter of right out of public revenue rather than depend on a game of chance, and expressing all too clearly the values of the something-for-nothing, get-rich-quick culture within which the ultimate in human happiness and the sum of all ambitions are represented by winning the roll-over jackpot.

It all adds up to what J. K. Galbraith has called 'the culture of contentment'; but in reality it carries within it the deepest discontent, so many signs of personal alienation and frustration, the still widening gap between rich and poor, producing increasing discrimination, marginalisation and social exclusion, together with a thoroughly regrettable narrowness of vision and meanness of spirit. The deputy editor of the excellent Glasgow daily paper *The Herald*, Alf Young, in his weekly column of 27 March 1998, said of this situation, with

Cassandra-like echoes once again of the twin phenomena of moral pluralism and values formed and driven by profit and productivity:

> At no point in my life has it been harder to define what we mean by a civic core. In this age of private finance initiatives, when commercial imperatives are being introduced to the very heart of the civic realm, it gets harder and harder to see what – other than the disciplines of the market-place – binds us together in a common sense of purpose or a shared vision of the good.

But this is not only a domestic, or even European condition. With modern technology and immensely improved communications the world has truly shrunk; distances and time differences are of little consequence, and the activities of transnational corporations have assumed a significance that surpasses the influence of all but the most powerful national governments. And yet paradoxically, as a recent study by the International Institute for Strategic Studies pointed out, 'The cold war tendency to see core interests indirectly at stake in distant parts of the globe has now totally eroded. Comfortably cocooned in their own sense of security, citizens of democratic countries are in no mood to sacrifice their well-being for supposed international advantage, nor to rally to the service of a purely humanitarian goal.'

Against the background of such rather cynical perceptions, there is an almost commonplace tendency within radical circles to attack, often with the fullest justification, the process of globalisation – as the sinister take-over of world power by unaccountable multinational corporations which pursue their own interests to the particular detriment of nations, and groups within them, that are already disadvantaged. But there are encouraging contrary forces at work motivated by generosity, and an impulse towards sharing together, something other than the narrow, primarily short-term interests that are so often apparently dominant. Not the least of these is the Jubilee 2000 campaign, seeking the relief of the international debt owed by the world's poorest nations, which has attracted much support in many countries. It is a salutary alternative to some of the other schemes for marking the Millennium, whether the excessively extravagant dome at Greenwich (surely the ultimate white elephant?) or the predominantly church-centred projects to which so much energy within the churches is being devoted.

Alongside the rise of consumerism, we have witnessed and suffered from the erosion of the sense of civic and communal responsibility and the apparently deliberate dismantling of public services through an ideological commitment to privatisation which the 1997 General Election scarcely seems to have halted. The considerations hinted at earlier in relation to the National Lottery apply here too: are such services to be regarded as a right, a matter of public responsibility, to be paid for through communal taxation; or are they rather commodities subject to all the practices and constraints of the market-place? No longer are we passengers, patients, students – all customers; the accountants have taken over the hospitals, the universities, the BBC, local government; and the big question now, the truly spiritual question, is whether the system of democratic market capitalism, the kind of mixed economy which will inevitably outlast changing governments, has sufficient flexibility to accommodate and express values like mutuality and generosity – or whether the culture of contractual relationships that has been introduced and developed is unredeemable.

Against this background, maybe even because of this background, many people are looking for something more substantial to set their sights on, stake their lives on, than the transitory, tawdry preoccupations and priorities that tend to take up so much of our time and effort and yet are ultimately empty. Many more people than we imagine today are looking deep down in their inmost hearts essentially for faith – a faith that touches, reassures and inspires them, that is credible, fulfilling and relevant to their needs and lives. There are so many signs of this quest for spirituality, meaning and depth – which is none other than a hunger for God – not least in the day-to-day contacts through the Iona Community's work both on the mainland and on Iona. Even people who are self-confessed atheists express concern for the spiritual well-being of society. (It should perhaps be added that my own experience, both in university chaplaincy and elsewhere, makes me hesitant about accepting the category of 'atheist' – often this is really a matter of semantics, involving little more than a rejection of a very simplistic understanding of God which would not be shared by many Christians – when in reality there is a passionate concern for and belief in issues of meaning, value, depth, even life-energy that would be associated with a modern understanding of God.)

And yet the churches seem to be facing something of a crisis with declining numbers and signs of uncertainty about their role in modern society. But at the same time there is continuing evidence that religion is alive in other ways, with opinion polls producing results of up to 80 per cent of the population still saying they believe in God. And there are many signs, as already mentioned, of individuals asking what life is all about, exploring ways other than through the institutional churches, and particularly through the voluntary sector perhaps, of pursuing their search for a sense of belonging and expressing their interest in spirituality and social concern. The influence of the churches has, at least in the eyes of some, reached such a low ebb that some commentators regard institutional religion and even the promotion of religious education in schools as inimical to the development of social cohesion in a pluralistic context: 'The decline of organised Christianity is a truth which we will have to accept if we are to build a more tolerant and more cohesive society. I suspect that in this country more people now go to mosques, gurdwaras, temples and synagogues on Fridays and Saturdays than turn up at churches and chapels on Sundays' (Roy Hattersley, *Guardian*, 7 April 1998).

One of George MacLeod's many striking sayings was that the trouble with the Church these days is that no one any longer thinks it is worth persecuting. The Church is regarded not with hostility, so much as with something like amused tolerance, or perhaps indifference and apathy. Especially by the young, but also increasingly among the middle-aged, it is seen as of marginal relevance to the realities of life – and only for the ultra-committed, the eccentric, or the weak. There is no longer any point and little attraction in belonging, whereas not so long ago holding office in the Church was a mark of social status, even a qualification for social advancement. It is essentially an issue of credibility, socially, intellectually, and indeed morally. The ethos and style of life of the Church are perceived by many as being out of date and out of touch. In the face of their personal priorities and preoccupations most people see no need for the Church, except perhaps in crises or as a social convenience for the rites of passage; they may want it to be there but they do not see any continuing personal significance or purpose in being involved.

The Church is perceived as of no consequence in relation to the pressing social and political issues of the day, and is perhaps expected to say rather old-fashioned, negative things about sex, drink, gambling, but with little helpful to contribute on the big social and economic questions. And there may also be the notion that somehow science has disproved religion or at least that commitment to the Church demands the acceptance of a package of beliefs that are not quite intellectually respectable. For many too the Church's language and music, its whole ritual and order of priorities is seen to be rooted in an alien culture that is out of line with the familiar currency of daily life. For others the objections may be on moral grounds so that the Church is rejected for ostensibly failing to live up to its own ideals, for being allegedly hypocritical, cold and judgmental rather than warm, open, welcoming and loving. The context is, to say the least, challenging: the spiritual questions and opportunities are there. But against this background, these perceptions and prejudices, what place can the Church have, whether as provider, as some would have it, of 'social glue', seeking to hold communities together, or as pointer to deeper realities for which some may be searching but others may not wish to acknowledge?

And where in the middle of all this is spirituality to be discovered and explored? The familiar T. S. Eliot phrase – 'the still point of the turning world' – provides a clear and helpful signpost, just as the Lipchitz statue, referred to in the previous chapter, does in the centre of the cloisters on Iona. God is in the midst; Jesus Christ reveals the central truth about the human condition; the Holy Spirit is in and through all things. Bewildering as the rate of change of the world around as may be in so many aspects, the heartbeat of God's love and the promise of the fullness of the kingdom remain constant. Amid the flux, how do we hold on, and what do we hold on to? Where is our journey going, through what territory, familiar or uncharted, is it to be pursued, and who will our companions be? It is with questions like these that the Iona Community has always grappled in attempting to develop an approach to its work that reflects above all a spirituality of engagement.

The social commentators and sociologists may talk learnedly of paradigm shifts and explain the significance of what is happening around us in terms of the rise of postmodernism, as described earlier, with its intrinsic distrust of objective authority and precipitate readiness to accord an exaggerated measure of validity to the impressions and experience of everyone and anyone. And yet it is undeniably true that it is not only in the eyes, minds and hearts of the young that the old certainties, the institutions that have seemed essential to the structure of society, are under challenge and showing signs of breaking down. People's perceptions, preoccupations and priorities have shifted significantly; society is secularised, religion demythologised and the sense of communal responsibility hugely diluted: 'The ethic of individual self-fulfilment and achievement is the most powerful current in modern society. Choosing, deciding, shaping individuals who aspire to be the authors of their lives, the creators their identities, are the central characters of our time' (Ulrich Beck, 'The Cosmopolitan Manifesto', in *The Herald*, 28 March 1998). From the family at local level to Parliament on the national scale, traditional institutions, including the Church and institutionalised religion, are proving inadequate to the tensions and pressures of today and no longer appear fully to meet people's needs. Within the political field the sense of disillusionment and alienation from existing structures of government is expressed both in electoral apathy, especially among the young, and in the emergence of a new kind of political culture, the birth of 'civil society' built on alliances and coalitions of a whole range of organisations with a common agenda.

And in the personal field, as a recent book review in the *Observer* put it (reflecting on the interest in and demand for psychoanalysis in terms of people's self-awareness as 'the failed artist of their own lives'), 'We used to look for our home on earth through God and religion, then through nature. Now therapy offers the final chance of belonging – be at home with yourself, in your own labyrinthine mind.' Again, it has been suggested that the rise of the so-called 'creative industries', involving people in literary and artistic occupations, from writers or artists in residence to design consultants and cultural project employees, is attributable to a combination of the approach of the millennium and a deep 'socio-pathological' sense of restlessness: 'people are less inclined to do ordinary jobs as they head towards an extraordinary mystical deadline. What we are witnessing is the occupational equivalent of partying until dawn'! (*Observer*, 19 April 1998). Or, at another level, countering the tendency to increasingly specialised, narrow, fragmented and compartmentalised views in the fields of both religion and science, there are signs of the development of an inclusive epistemology, the kind of world-vision in and through which there is convergence between such disciplines as astronomy, theoretical physics, theology, philosophy, and the higher reaches of mathematics. This is seen for example in Stephen Hawking's best-selling *A Brief History of Time*, with its enigmatic reference to God in the closing section, in Edward Wilson's recent exploration of the term 'consilience', dating from the Enlightenment and referring literally to the jumping together of different aspects of knowledge, or in the work of the American Fritjof Capra who speaks in *The Turning Point* of 'a new vision of reality, a fundamental change in our thoughts, perceptions and values'. This is said to involve a holistic approach drawing on a whole variety of disciplines, pointing to the interconnectedness of experience, the integrity of knowledge and the unity of truth – offering a more hopeful way forward, assuming the existence of an over-arching 'meta-narrative' that is at least partially accessible, than most of the apostles of postmodernism and deconstructionism. So, in a variety of ways, the search for meaning and depth, the quest for roots and identity, goes on, and it is taking people in new directions, looking for the kind of mountain-top experiences with which this chapter started.

As I hope has become increasingly clear I believe that, however they may be expressed, such issues ultimately have to do with spirituality, even if many would resist the introduction into their discussion of what may be regarded as patently 'religious' words or concepts such as 'faith' or 'God'. And alongside the level of philosophising in the realm of ideas there is a strong personal dimension. Much of this quest for spirituality is in fact an exercise in self-development, achieving a sense of inner connectedness, belonging within oneself, a compulsion towards a kind of 'psychosomatic integrity' involving little more than what has been called, with appropriate dismissiveness, 'designer spirituality', without any recognition of the significance of the social dimension – that fulfilment and fullness of life will only be discovered as an individual *in community*. Equally, in the specifically religious context, the quest can all too easily end up in a kind of pietistic, individualised detachment, reflecting often in a thoroughly sentimental fashion both the dominant ethos of our times, as we have seen, and the preoccupation with the personal.

Last year the Social Affairs Unit, for long a mouthpiece and think-tank of the New Right, published a book *Faking It: The Sentimentalism of Modern Society* that evoked considerable comment from some of the social commentators. In essence it was a diatribe against the feel-good society, the dominance of sentimentality that denies and degrades real feelings in favour of a kind of self-absorbed and self-indulgent fantasising. It condemned 'the elevation of feeling, image, spontaneity over reason, reality, and restraint'. What is at issue here of course is a question of balance: wholeness is achieved, whether within an individual life or within a community, when reason and feeling, head and heart are well integrated, work together and are combined in appropriate measure.

It is not hard to see the connections between all this and the preoccupation with spirituality, which can so easily take people up blind alleys and in directions that are not at all helpful or enriching. What is clearly called for is a process that may be described as balanced discernment, that is able to see the need for both reason and emotion, that can distinguish show from substance, semblance from reality. Indeed the Iona Community's experience shows quite certainly that one of the principal attractions of Iona is the nostalgic, romantic search for peace and tranquillity, related so often to the escapist pursuit of a mistaken Celtic ideal. As already said in the previous chapter, personal spiritual fulfilment, and the practices and discipline associated with it, are indisputably important – the 'be still and know that I am God' approach, which is reflective and contemplative. This, however, does not constitute or represent the whole of spirituality: and in Chapter 9 we shall explore this more fully; but the essence of the Iona Community's approach, reflecting a fundamental strand of the Christian tradition that has its roots within the theology of the Old Testament and which was a strong theme too within Celtic Christianity, is that 'God is in the midst', truly in and through all things, and spirituality is therefore essentially about *engagement*, 'a multi-faceted centredness in the life of the spirit with a clear social dimension and expression' (*What is the Iona Community?)*

Kenneth Leech sums all this up very effectively in *The Eye of the Storm*:

> Spirituality can be a dangerous diversion from the living God, from the demands of justice, from engagement with reality. It can be a form of illusion . . . Today 'spirituality' is marketed as a product, in competition with others, on the station bookstalls. It belongs to the area of 'private life' . . . Of all the distortions of Christian faith and discipleship, it is individualism that has most penetrated spiritual consciousness . . . At its very heart the Christian life and identity is a process of incorporation into a new social organism, a new community. Spirituality cannot exist apart from this social context.

O God, gladly we live and move and have our being in you.
Yet always in the midst of this creation-glory,
We see sin's shadow and feel death's darkness:
Around us in the earth, sea and sky the abuse of matter;
Beside us in the broken, the hungry and the poor,
The betrayal of one another;
And often, deep within us, a striving against your Spirit.
O Trinity of love,

Forgive us that we may forgive one another,
Heal us that we may be people of healing,
And renew us that we also may be makers of peace.

(George MacLeod (adapted),
The Iona Community Worship Book)

Creator God,
weaver of the world in all its variety,
you know our warp and weft: where we cross,
the diverse colours of our opinion, the textures of our faith,
you feel our quality,
you touch our frayed edges,
you accept us:
you love us, different as we are –
Thank you.

Christ of the seamless robe,
again and again we strip you
and cast lots, arguing over material things,
missing the meaning of ministry,
averting our eyes from the cross,
failing to be your body in the world –
Forgive us.

Holy Spirit, networking in the church,
forming our loose ends into a fishing net,
where the strands hold hands around the holes,
making our daily work a sign of God's work in the world,
sign of our connectedness,
sign of our calling:
help us to hold together
and to draw others into your kingdom –
Use us. Amen

(Jan Sutch Pickard, *Vice Versa*)

3

The Iona Community – Celebrating Spirituality

In 1988, the year of the Iona Community's Golden Jubilee, a special edition of the Community's magazine *Coracle* was produced, containing alongside much historical material some reflections on the challenges and opportunities facing the Community over the time ahead, including the following comment by Ron Ferguson, then Leader of the Community:

> The need for a supportive network of people committed to radical spirituality and radical politics will grow, and it will require to operate both within and outwith the institutional church . . . God has provided resources for us beyond our limited imaginings. The resources are there for a purpose – building and rebuilding the common life. The task is urgent, not only in the Third World but in a Britain whose values are being rolled back, not just to the 1930s, but to the Victorian era.

The past couple of years have involved the Iona Community

in the celebration of further significant anniversaries. The summer of 1997 was particularly busy on Iona itself, with an additional influx of day visitors and parish groups undertaking special pilgrimages to mark the 1400th anniversary of the death of Columba and a whole series of requests, gladly complied with, to hold musical and dramatic events, including several premières, focusing on the life of Columba. The English churches, with the Church of England taking a strong lead, were keen to celebrate the coming of Augustine to England, also in 597, and the Scottish churches in turn, through the ecumenical body Action of Churches Together in Scotland (ACTS) were ready to share in a joint initiative, which fitted in well for their own plans for a special four-year programme towards the turn of the century. So a major ecumenical pilgrimage was planned, starting at Canterbury, Augustine's own base, travelling by three separate routes, one through Wales, another by Whithorn in Galloway, and a third by Lindisfarne and Iona, all visiting places of religious and historical significance and finishing together at Derry, near Columba's birthplace on Columba's Day, 9 June. Within Scotland 1997 was designated the 'Year of Faith', and also the 'Year of the Saints' – Ninian (whom many believe to have arrived at Whithorn, in Galloway, in 397, although most recent scholarship casts doubt on the authenticity of this precise date), as well as Columba and Augustine.

The Iona Community for its part decided, in view of the considerable pressure on its islands centres and staff in a 'normal' year (and also perhaps because in 1963 the Community had put a huge effort into marking the 1400th anniversary of Columba's *arrival* on Iona – possibly a more significant occasion than his death!), that large-scale celebrations on Iona were out of the question. It encouraged Members and Associates of the Community, however, in conjunction where possible with local councils of churches and churches and schools bearing the name of Columba, to explore the possibility of holding worship and other events in their own locality around Columba's Day, and produced, through the Wild Goose Resource Group, liturgical material as a resource for such services. They also commissioned Ian Bradley, author of what many believe to be the most helpful introduction to Celtic Christianity – *The Celtic Way* – to write a book about Columba and his significance for our times – *Columba, Pilgrim and Penitent* – and included in the 1997 Iona summer programme a special week, with Columba and the continuing relevance of the Celtic tradition as its theme.

That turned out to be a memorable week – one to be survived as well as relished! In addition to the usual programme, led by Ian Bradley in immensely stimulating fashion, there was even less time than usual for guests and staff to relax since it seemed that each day had its own extra events and special visitors. There was a concentration of the artistic premières, already mentioned, choral, orchestral and dramatic, fitted into some of the gaps between the regular Abbey services. There was a whole series of special services – the ecumenical pilgrimage passing through *en route* for Ireland, the St Columba's Day service full of distinctive music and symbolism, the Scottish Episcopal Church prior to a General Synod at Oban, and a Triduum of Prayer arranged by the Scottish Roman Catholic Church attracting bus-loads of pilgrims from parishes all over Scotland over three days. And the pilgrims came from near and far, by land and sea, most movingly a group who battled against the elements to row all the way from Ireland and who arrived just in time for the Sunday morning Communion service, and a flotilla of yachtsman who sailed through very stormy weather to make the Columba Day service. But the greatest excitement and the highest tension involved, on a single day, a live broadcast and a visit by a Head of State! In a sense there had been a dress rehearsal the previous year, when the Princess Royal, as the Queen's formal representative at the Church of Scotland's General Assembly in May had visited

Iona to see the Community's work there. The Community was greatly honoured that Mrs Mary Robinson, then President of Ireland, accepted an invitation from the Community to come to Iona to mark the links between Iona and Ireland in the year of the Columban anniversary. They were also delighted that the BBC responded so positively to a suggestion concerning broadcast worship with live services on Radio Scotland, Radio 4 and Radio 3 and a tele-recorded *Songs of Praise.*

The experience of 1997 was thoroughly enjoyable, especially in retrospect, but not to be repeated the following year even though 1998 was the Community's sixtieth anniversary. So a fairly muted low-key approach was adopted by contrast with the arrangements the previous year. There were a couple of publications – a series of meditations and biblical reflections (first published in *Coracle*) by Ian Reid, Leader of the Community after George MacLeod, who had died in February 1997; and a revised edition of Ron Ferguson's highly readable history of the Community *Chasing the Wild Goose.* And the Abbey programme contained a week, entitled rather pretentiously 'The Diamond and the Dreams', providing an opportunity to reflect on not only the Community's history but also the current concerns and future priorities. It turned out to be an excellent week, with people from many different countries sharing insights and experiences in exploring their own journeys against the background of the Community's story.

The programme at the centres on Iona regularly includes a session for guests on 'What is the Iona Community?' and often starts off with a film called *Sermon in Stone*. Made over thirty years ago, shortly after the completion of the rebuilding of the Abbey, the film now inevitably seems dated in several respects and tends to be regarded with affectionate amusement by many Community Members, a good number of whom have seen it so many times that they more or less know the commentary off by heart and love to parody it. But the film is also very impressive and extremely moving. The script is written and delivered by George MacLeod, still clearly in his prime. There is original colour footage from the 1930s, and with skilful integration of visual material and soundtrack it appears to have been a pioneering piece of work, ahead of its time. But its main interest clearly is for the account it gives of the history and work of the Community – and it is highly significant for the present purpose that the word 'spirituality' does not appear once.

Similarly the word hardly occurs in the early editions of *Coracle*, the foundation documents of the Community, mostly written by George MacLeod himself as a combination of promotional material, to attract interest and support, or as defence, often correcting misunderstandings, rebutting allegations, explaining the Community and its purposes for the benefit of its opponents and critics. But the absence of any explicit reference to spirituality is simply a reflection of the culture of the times. The Community has always tended to describe its approach in terms of incarnational theology – the Word becoming flesh and thereby bridging the gap between sacred and secular, embodying the integration of spiritual and material. Indeed the Community owes its origins to this very gap, strikingly evident among the shipyards of Govan, the highly industrialised Clydeside parish in Glasgow where George MacLeod was minister in the 1930s. Except insofar as it has a bearing on exploring the Community's understanding of and approach to spirituality this is not the place to rehearse other than in outline the story of the Community which is so well told by Ron Ferguson (Leader of the Community from 1981 to 1988) in *Chasing the Wild Goose* and his biography of George MacLeod, and by Ralph Morton in *The Iona Community: Personal Impressions of the Early Years*.

In many people's eyes Govan Old was a 'successful' church and George MacLeod an effective minister, active in the local community, pastorally sensitive and approachable, attracting large congregations. But he felt that the Church was not addressing or meeting people's real needs, was out of touch with the ordinary people. He saw the need for new approaches relevant to the demands of the contemporary situation, new approaches to mission, especially in the working areas where the Church and the Gospel seemed to be making little impact, and new approaches to training ministers. George MacLeod already knew Iona well. The restoration of the Abbey church had been completed in 1910 by the Cathedral Trustees to whom the Duke of Argyll had passed responsibility for the buildings on condition that, although the Trustees have formal links with the Church of Scotland, the church would be open for worship of all denominations. Now George MacLeod with immense vision and energy developed and carried through a scheme for the restoration of the rest of the monastic buildings, the living quarters, the cloisters, the ancillary chapels. At the time, in the economic depression of the 1930s and with the storm clouds of war gathering, here was a visible, tangible sign of hope. The story of how George MacLeod did this has its own intrinsic interest, and as in the best oral traditions it has been well embellished through transmission down the years. What is of significance here is above all the underlying thinking and the sense of purpose that guided and inspired the project – for the process was as important as the intended outcome and reflected from the very outset of the Iona Community, when the rebuilding started in 1938, the same integrated approach to spirituality which undergirds the activities of the Community to this day, even if it was articulated rather differently then.

The rebuilding of the Abbey was to be a learning experience. A group of craftsmen was assembled, and alongside them young ministers. They grew together as a community, never an easy experience; and they grew in mutual understanding and learned from one another – about the world of work, about the relevance of prayer and worship, how to communicate the Gospel in a down-to-earth accessible way. Worship and work flowed in and out of one another in a way that was entirely natural; the pattern of the days revealed that life cannot be compartmentalised, the sacred separated off from the secular; the lively conversation and discussions reflected the mutual interpenetration of interest and commitment in the fields of politics and religion.

All the evidence suggests that George MacLeod did not initially intend the Iona Community to have a continuing existence. A community would form each summer for the rebuilding work and the men would then go back to work on the mainland, the ministers in demanding urban parishes to explore new strategies and patterns of ministry and mission; and a new community would then be recruited for the succeeding year's work. But the Iona experience proved so rich and deep that many of those involved wished to hold on to the reality of belonging together; hence the emergence of the Iona Community as it is still known, not an 'intentional', living together kind of community, but rather a dispersed community, in some ways more akin to a religious order in the traditional sense, with a base or 'home' on Iona, but rooted, earthed and engaged in a whole range of different local situations.

The rebuilding of the Abbey was completed in 1967 and at that point many people asked what the Iona Community was going to do now. Their question, of course, betrayed a failure to understand that the Abbey was only an outward sign of a deeper reality, at the spiritual level. The basic purpose of the Community continued – continues still – to contribute to a process of rebuilding that goes on and on, God's renewal and reshaping of individual lives, of the Church and of wider society. Over the years there have inevitably been many changes of emphasis and priorities, but the main thrusts of the work have been constant; and the themes explored in the *Sermon in Stone* film remain frighteningly relevant more than thirty years on! For over twenty years, from the 1950s to the late 1970s, Community House in Clyde Street, Glasgow was a familiar landmark for many, embodying the Community's commitment to the life of the city, both 'a sanctuary and a light', as one of the Community's prayers puts it in relation to the significance of the Abbey on Iona. Until its closure in the late 1970s, partly for redevelopment reasons, partly because changes in the social and cultural environment had reduced the demand for the services and facilities it offered, for over thirty years Community House played a large part in the development of youth and community work in the west of Scotland. It did so with a diverse range of pioneering educational activities including drama and politics, and the provision of social services; it also housed several other voluntary organisations and the importance of both its chapel and its café speak here too of the integrated, engaged spirituality. Since the mid-1980s the Community's mainland base and administrative headquarters have been in the Pearce Institute in Govan close to Govan Old Parish Church which George MacLeod left to found the Community.

It is interesting that over a period when the membership of the Church has been declining, the Iona Community has experienced considerable growth. *Sermon in Stone* refers to a membership of 140, with 800 Associate Members and 4000 Friends; in 1998 the corresponding figures are 211 Members, over 1500 Associate Members and around 1700 Friends, with every sign that those in the first two of these categories (comprising people who wish to make a significant commitment to supporting the work and concerns of the Community) will continue to grow. From anecdotal evidence this would appear to be attributable to a substantial extent to the Community's inclusive and integrated approach to spirituality. Among the Members there has been a gradually widening denominational affiliation, with all the mainstream churches in Britain now represented, although Church of Scotland is still the largest single denomination. Ordained ministers are now in a minority – there is a very broad range of occupational backgrounds –

and there are almost as many women as men, although it was 1969 before the first woman Member was admitted. In the 1960s there were around forty Members overseas – more than one-third of the membership at the time; now there are only a dozen. This reflects changing patterns in overseas mission rather than any lessening of commitment on the Community's part to the important process of sharing in the world-wide work of the Church. This is readily apparent, for example, in the Community's prayers, liturgical themes, pursuit of justice and peace issues, and the number of Iona staff who come from overseas.

Over recent years the Community has supported a number of mainland projects that seek to reflect its corporate concerns. These have changed in the light of the needs of the time and also of personalities and perceived priorities; but there has been a general consistency of purpose and a recognition also that reaching out in faith and with spiritual insight demands both a readiness to take risks and a strong sense of provisionality. Various workers and schemes have, as it were, come and gone, involving, for example, the exploration of work issues, local community outreach, a youth volunteer programme, a lay training project, the support of a full-time justice and peace worker, and the development of 'Columban Houses', small communities where people associated with the Community and its concerns shared a common life of hospitality, worship and mutual support. Through all of these, and reflected also in various aspects of the communal life at the islands centres (and in particular in the shared leadership of worship), there has run for many years a strong commitment to the ministry of the whole people of God. This field of the development of lay ministry was where Ralph Morton, who was first Warden of Community House in Glasgow, and Deputy Leader to George MacLeod for many years, made a particularly valuable contribution, not only within the Community, but in pointing to opportunities and possibilities within the life of the churches generally, most notably perhaps through his authorship, with Mark Gibbs, of *God's Frozen People*. In this connection also, among the many networks with which the Community is linked, are associations of centres, within both Britain and Europe, with an emphasis on lay training.

Another continuing priority since fairly early in the Community's lifetime has been the commitment to youth work, with a staff member appointed specifically to co-ordinate and develop the Community's concern in this area, although there have been changes from time to time in detailed responsibilities and in how this is organised. In recent years additional effort and resources have been devoted to the fields of publishing (in which the Community has been engaged from the outset, both through pamphlets, books, and *Coracle*, the Community's regular magazine whose form has gone through several changes over the years) and worship, with the Wild Goose Resource and Worship Groups gaining a reputation for innovative and participative approaches and the development of songs and other worship resources that are more accessible than much of the traditional material.

On Iona too there have been significant changes that reflect the themes of seeking to build community, finding new ways of making faith come alive and holding together social and spiritual concerns. In the early 1970s it was decided that the Abbey should be staffed by a resident group, with the assistance of shorter-term volunteers, all under the leadership of a Warden, and this model has been developed and expanded to meet the increasing demand for places on the week-long programmes. In 1988 the MacLeod Centre was opened with facilities specially suited for families and groups of younger people and access for disabled people that cannot readily be provided in a historic building like the Abbey. It stands on the site occupied for many years by the youth camp, made up of the huts originally used to house those rebuilding the Abbey which had reached a state beyond repair. Before that in turn, the

Community's youth work on Iona had been carried out in huts and under canvas, remembered with great affection by many as 'The Village Camp' and 'The North End Camp'.

The centre at Camas on Mull is reached by a half-hour walk across a moorland track a couple of miles from Fionnphort from which the Iona ferry runs. Camas, originally a row of quarrymen's cottages, until recently still operating as a salmon-fishing station, has also been consolidated and developed over the years. Initially used by George MacLeod in the early days of the Community for Borstal groups, it entered a new phase in the 1970s under dedicated and imaginative leadership and now fulfils a distinctive role within the life of the Community, catering especially for groups with special needs and disadvantaged situations, and adds an important dimension to the Community's approach to spirituality with its emphasis on the outdoors, the adventurous and its awareness of the significance of the environment.

Aspects of the work of the Community thus may have changed over the years but the core values and central purpose persist. As later chapters will explore more fully, there is continuing debate and discussions among the Members about future priorities and how we belong together. More than sixty years on, to what extent has the Community become institutionalised, a familiar part of the scenery as it were? And is it possible therefore that we have lost some of our radical cutting edge and our ability to explore issues of spirituality in a truly open fashion? Or is it our very rootedness, the fact that we carry the 'baggage' of these sixty years which enables us to explore these issues with all the more responsibility and authenticity? How, other than at the most superficial level, do we continue to 'belong together', know and relate closely to one another, own responsibility as individual Members for the corporate decisions?

We frequently refer to our identity as both organisation and movement and all the ambiguities and paradoxes that entails, but we keep telling ourselves that these tensions are creative! With the Community's very significant growth over recent years, with more staff and increased budgets, our committee structures and decision-making processes have been streamlined and made much less cumbersome. Whereas twenty years ago, with smaller numbers, many decisions were made at plenary meetings of Community Members (often thus highly emotionally charged and uncomfortable occasions!), these gatherings are now primarily opportunities for celebrating and exploring together, catching up with one another and reflecting on various topics of common concern sometimes within the life of the Community, more often in the wider world. The Community as a whole tends to reach decisions only on the matters of the most strategic significance (for instance on whether to build the MacLeod Centre or move to a new mainland base); most matters are delegated to the committees – Council (the executive committee) and specific committees with responsibilities for finance and staffing, islands work, mainland work, and publishing – who set the policy framework within which staff are accountable for the detailed day-to-day decisions.

Along with the expansion and increase in scale several interesting issues have arisen. For instance, staff numbers have grown substantially: between Glasgow and Iona (including Camas) there are now almost fifty people on contracts, the requirements relating to staff management and more detailed employment legislation have to be met, and attention has to be given to the need for effective and sensitive support arrangements for staff, both on the islands and the mainland. There is also what might be described as the vocational issue: some staff members are Community Members, others are Associate Members, others again, while in sympathy with the general aims of the Community, may see their working for the Community simply as a congenial and worthwhile job without identifying themselves with the Community in any formal way, or indeed even professing any Christian commitment. While the preparation and review of the Community's strategic plan over the last ten years or so attempted to lead to a process that reconciled the Community's 'two natures' as organisation and movement, through the identification of agreed priorities and the development of structures that struck a good balance between the principles of participation and delegation, continuing attention has to be given to the importance of effective communication lest there be any sense, on the part of individual Members, of being out of touch with what is going on and with decisions that are being taken. Clearly there must be a high degree of mutual trust, and the Community's commitment to accountability is fundamental.

The discussion of structures may at first sight seem a far cry from spirituality. And yet the whole basis of the Community's understanding is that everything has spiritual significance; God can and does work through committees! Movements need to be organised and organisations require direction, energy and impetus if they are to go anywhere and do anything. Over recent years the Community has become increasingly aware of the importance of process. The experience often matters as much as the outcome, the journey as the reaching of the goal; how one does something is as relevant as what is achieved. With the increase in scale and the need for consistency and accountability it is true that there may be a danger of creating or being absorbed almost unwittingly into a world of bureaucracy. Good practice and good order are necessary to the communal well-being and to individual flourishing but this does not automatically lead to an approach that relies on rules and regulations that operate like straitjackets: there must also be the element of flexibility and imagination that leaves room for creativity and growth. And what all this adds up to has to do with the integration and connectedness that is the root of healthy spirituality.

While it is ultimately the responsibility of the Leader of the

Community to 'hold it all together', much weight is placed on corporate processes and regular staff meetings – with responsibility exercised on Iona through a management team and resident liaison group, and in Glasgow through a liaison group and monthly staff meeting. When George MacLeod was Leader, as both Founder and a highly charismatic figure, he was able to pursue a style that was very much more autocratic than is at all possible now. There is no way now (nor has there been for some considerable time) that a Community of strong-willed, extraordinarily gifted and committed people will submit to going in any direction they do not wish to follow. Ian Reid, George MacLeod's successor as Leader, described his task as trying to control 140 wild horses all pulling in different directions – and since then the membership is half as big again. The Leader is both co-ordinator and front-man, required at times to be preacher and pastor, with a special, formidable responsibility to both nurture and facilitate the development of the vision, called to care for something that is both fragile and precious, but carries with it also a sense of risk and unpredictability, what might be described perhaps as the 'wild goose' dimension.

George MacLeod first referred to the wild goose as a Celtic symbol for the Holy Spirit in one of the early editions of *Coracle.* It was in the 1980s that the wild goose was adopted, under copyright, in the form of an intricate, unending Celtic design, as the official 'logo' of the Community; and now the Community's publishing department has a separate identity as Wild Goose Publications, the Community's outreach workers who specialise in worship are the Wild Goose Resource Group, and in the Abbey shop the Community sells a whole range of products, from china to attractive brooches, with the wild goose design.

Recent attempts, in consultation with various Celtic scholars, have failed entirely to establish the authenticity of the symbol within the Celtic tradition; and the lack of more than the vaguest evidence suggests that, like much else within the Community's story, it may have been a product of George MacLeod's rich and fertile imagination! It is, however, a tribute to his insight that there are enough associations and indications around to hint at the possibility that it might be genuine. An old Celtic cross from Aberlady, in East Lothian, now in the National Museum of Antiquities of Scotland, depicts a large bird that might very well be a wild goose; there are strands of Celtic mythology where the wild goose is recognised as a messenger of the gods (rather like Hermes/Mercury within classical mythology), not dissimilar to the understanding of the Holy Spirit as advocate or representative of God; and, from another religious tradition entirely – leading one to wonder whether the image results from George MacLeod's travels to many parts of the world on behalf of the Community, the wild goose does represent the spirit of the gods within the Hindu faith.

In fact the debate on the issue of authenticity may be of some academic interest but has little contemporary relevance otherwise. Whatever its origin the symbol of the wild goose has a rich depth and powerful, helpful connotations. Over the last twenty years or so, the Community's discussions and the pages of *Coracle* have been further enlivened from time to time by wild goose sightings in many unexpected places – whether through fleeting reference in a casual snatch of conversation or more deliberate literary illusion or artefact. *Chasing the Wild Goose* highlights some of the characteristics which reach right to the heart of the Community's life, illuminate our own experience, in reminding us, for instance, that geese in formation can fly much faster and farther than they do individually. In some eyes of course wild geese are regarded as disturbing nuisances, creating noise at moments that are often inconvenient, even pests to be shot. And at another level the goose image conveys a sense of foolishness (with the pointers this can provide to the upside-down values of God's kingdom), even of awkwardness, at least on the ground. But in flight the wild goose has grace and beauty, conveys a sense of the unpredictable and the untamable, and in the strength of the beat of its great wings there is exceptional power and the capacity to achieve the apparently impossible. Put all this together and the wild goose image has a deep resonance, indeed in terms of spirituality, with the energy, direction, and vulnerability of the Community.

In the Golden Jubilee *Coracle* of 1988 Ron Ferguson echoed the sentiments of many Community Members when he said, 'The movement is a work of faith – it will continue as long as God requires it.' That may sound rather glib and pious, even to smack of a more deterministic theology than most Members would subscribe to intellectually: nonetheless in our hearts and guts we believe it! But in the meantime we find it immensely encouraging and reassuring that so many people, sometimes in remarkably surprising and unexpected quarters, clearly still see a role for the Community.

On Iona especially, but in discussions elsewhere also, I am often asked how the Community has managed to sustain its vision and commitment in face of the multifarious pressures and the inevitable setbacks and disappointments that, alongside the highpoints, have been experienced during the sixty years of its existence. There is no simple answer to this question of course; it has been done by the grace of God alone, at times with difficulty, always through the love, patience and constancy of so many Members and other supporters and well-wishers. But there is also the unshakable conviction that there is a job there to be done, the strong sense of calling to what Peter Millar described, in a paper prepared for Community Week 1998 with reflections on his experience as Warden on Iona from 1995 to 1998, as a ministry of 'prophetic awareness and pastoral action'.

Many Community Members have found inspiration in the writings of the American biblical scholar Walter Brueggemann. In *The Prophetic Imagination* he has written:

> The task of prophetic ministry is to nurture, nourish, and evoke a consciousness and perception alternative to the consciousness and perception of the dominant culture around us . . . The formation of an alternative community with an alternative consciousness is so that the dominant community may be criticised and finally dismantled . . . Jesus . . . practiced the energising of the new future given by God. This energising was fully wrought in his resurrection, in which he embodied the new future given by God.'

That expresses fairly well both the essence of the Iona Community's spirituality and what the Community has attempted to do and to be during its lifetime – with a degree of modesty and hesitancy perhaps, avoiding frills and pretensions, recognising that in our belonging together there must be both room and opportunity to celebrate and readiness to acknowledge our corporate and individual shortcomings and the flaws.

> The sense of belonging flows from trust: trust is the gradual acceptance of others as they are with their gifts and their limits, each one with the call of Jesus. And this leads to the realisation that the body of community is not perfectly whole and cannot be, that this is our human condition. And it is all right for us to be less than perfect. We must not weep over our imperfections. We are not judged for being defective. Our God knows that in so many ways we are lame and half blind. We will never win the olympics of humanity, racing for perfection, but we can walk together in hope, celebrating that we are loved in our brokenness:
>
> helping each other,
> growing in trust,
> living in thanksgiving,

learning to forgive,
opening up to others,
welcoming them,
and striving to bring peace and hope to our world. So it is that we come to put down roots in community not because it is perfect and wonderful, but because we believe that Jesus has called us together. It is where we belong and are called to grow and to serve. (Jean Vanier, *The Broken Body*)

O God our Father, who gave to your servant Columba the gifts of courage, faith and cheerfulness, and sent people forth from Iona to carry the word of your Gospel to every creature, grant, we pray, a like spirit to your church, even at this present time. Further in all things the purpose of our Community, that hidden things may be revealed to us, and new ways found to touch the hearts of all. May we preserve with each other sincere charity and peace, and, if it be your holy will, grant that a place of your abiding be continued still to be a sanctuary and a light, through Jesus Christ our Lord, Amen. (From the 'Office' of the Iona Community)

God, we thank you for all the light, grace and life seen and known in the church and community which nurtured us. Praying that still we may be set free from narrow-mindedness and complacency, open our eyes that we may recognise the work of your Spirit among other people and in different forms. And should we yet walk in some things on separate ways, then present before us the common goal towards which we travel.
(A prayer from the Swedish Church, (adapted),
The Wee Worship Book)

4

The Membership and Rule of the Community

I can well remember when first I visited Iona in 1968 just after our honeymoon in Ireland. In a sense I married into the Iona Community: my wife's parents, although neither was ever a Community Member, met while working with George MacLeod in Govan in the mid-1930s (my father-in-law as assistant minister, my mother-in-law as a social worker running girls' clubs), and they remained interested in and supportive of the Community throughout their lives; my wife's sister's husband was Warden in the Abbey and was later my predecessor as Leader, my wife's sister later became a Member herself, and my wife's twin brother has also been a Member since the 1960s.

My own interest was awakened from that first visit although I did not feel able to join the Community until 1980, after I left the civil service, where I spent the first fifteen years of my working life, after St Andrews University, in the Scottish Office, based in Edinburgh, but latterly spending much time around Westminster and Whitehall. But in the late 1960s I can remember my curiosity and fascination being aroused by these men in dark blue suits, lighter blue shirts and navy ties, by what I was told about the significance of membership, and by reports then that for the first time women also were being admitted. Changed days indeed now! The 'uniform' adopted in the early days, as an alternative to 'clerical grey', as a mark of identification and solidarity with industrial workers, has long been abandoned, although a few blue shirts and ties will still be in evidence at, for instance, the annual Hallowing service during Community Week on Iona in August, the only act of worship in the year when the Community Members sit separately in the Abbey choir stalls and crossing, with the rest of the congregation in the nave, as from six to a dozen or more people are 'hallowed' into full membership on completion of the two-year joining programme; and the service is followed by the Hallowing Supper, a splendid celebratory meal to which islanders and other guests are invited and the cloisters, transformed into the eating-space for the evening, resound with conversation and laughter. Since the 1960s there have been significant changes in the composition of the Community, with an increasing denominational spread, more and more English Members, the swing towards a majority of lay over ordained members, and there are now almost as many women as men.

But what interested me most, through these early contacts, was what impelled people to become Members and what held them together – issues once more of connectedness, energy and engagement: already, without really knowing it, I was probing and exploring the Community's approach to spirituality. During the last few Community Weeks on Iona in August one of the sessions has involved a 'dialogue', in small groups, between staff and Community Members, with the purpose of increasing mutual understanding and providing insights into the commitment involved both in working for and belonging to the Community. It is really an exploration in spirituality through sharing the feelings and experience of different situations, whether about working on Iona or why people become and remain Members. On the two most recent occasions the discussion started off with everyone present responding to the question 'what is important to me about the Iona Community?'. Among staff, alongside expressions of appreciation and some of the practical issues (both positive and negative), one of the recurring points was the paradox of carrying out the Community's corporate work in the public eye and often being perceived as 'the Iona Community' and yet not formally being Members; and this question of how staff relate and belong is being looked at further.

Among Members there were inevitably some strong common themes – the commitment to justice and peace, as a spiritual concern; the importance of the Rule, instilling some discipline, order and priorities in too busy, often chaotic lives; the sense of belonging together, of both challenge and support on people's personal journeys of witness and discipleship. To some extent it is a mystery, a result above all perhaps of personality and circumstances, why some people join the Community and others do not, remaining strong supporters, whether part of the Community's wider family of Associate Members and Friends or simply encouragers and well-wishers, as it were, from the sidelines. In many ways the Community is rather like a religious order, and as such many of those who are confused when they discover that the people living at and running our islands centres are not after all 'the Iona Community' find it easier to understand our common commitment, around the Rule and our shared concerns, and the Community's dispersed nature.

Similarly the programme for New Members is based on the same sort of idea as a religious order's novitiate (in the sense of testing commitment and exploring to what extent the hopes and expectations of the individual and the concerns and nature of the Community are compatible), although there are obviously huge practical differences in view of the totally different circumstances of those going through the process. There are no formal qualifications for membership of the Community. People are expected to have been Associate

Members normally for at least two years and to have some background, contact and experience of the Community, whether through involvement with Associates Groups, Family Groups, regular visits to Iona, working for the Community on Iona or the mainland or in other ways. A meeting takes place, involving the Leader of the Community and another Member as well as the applicant, not to determine whether the applicant comes up to the mark or fulfils some set criterion but to discuss the Community's work and explore the applicant's aspirations so as to ensure that from all points of view the time is right to start the programme.

From the outset the new Member has all the obligations and responsibilities of a full Member – with the exception of the right to stand for Council (the Community's executive committee) or the position as convener (chair) of one of the other committees and the right to vote at plenary meetings in elections or on other business issues. Thus new Members are expected to attend plenaries and their local Family Group meeting regularly and frequently, and so become integrated into the life of the Community and familiar with its concerns in a deeper way. In addition the New Members programme involves a series of five residential events over a two-year period, providing an opportunity for the building of community among the participants and for full discussion of the details and significance of different aspects of the Community's life and work – the Rule, the areas of concern identified as working priorities, how new Members' own journeys and experiences relate to the 'story' and processes of the Community, and so on. The time involved in attending these events represents a considerable commitment for most people, using holidays for this purpose, especially where there are family commitments. In addition to two Community Weeks on Iona, at which all are expected to be present, it amounts to one weekend for first-year new Members for what is euphemistically called the 'autumn gathering' (although it usually takes place in the depths of winter) held at different venues from year to year, and four weeks for all the new Members, one at a mainland centre, the other three at the Community's own centres, one on Iona just after Easter, and two work weeks at Camas. This last is invariably found to be an immensely enriching experience because of the simplicity of the life-style, the closeness and sensitivity to the environment, and the demanding character of the work (in recent years from gardening to carpentry, from stone-pointing to track-repairing, usually irrespective of the weather). New Members are also expected to undertake a 'mainland project', through which they may extend their awareness of some aspect of the Community's life with which they are less familiar. This is an opportunity as much as a binding obligation; it is not like a degree dissertation in that no one has 'failed' for not completing their task satisfactorily! But over recent years there have been some very imaginative and worthwhile projects – for example, a study in homelessness; photographic and artistic compilations; various activity-centred initiatives; a set of biblical reflections and prayers on justice and peace.

With the encouraging increase in interest in joining the Community a ceiling of twenty-four has had to be set for the New Members programme, both on account of the capacity of Camas and for considerations of group dynamics, although the number going through has been close to this figure for some time. In the course of the two-year period one or two people may drop out of the programme, usually because of difficulty in fulfilling the requirements of the programme alongside other continuing commitments; but for the great majority who complete the programme the Hallowing Service, when they are admitted to full membership, is both the culmination of a very rich and enjoyable experience, full of laughter, singing and memories that will linger for a long time, when insights are deepened and strong bonds of friendship and belonging together formed, and the beginning of a new, challenging stage of their spiritual journey.

Now, in the late 1990s, the Community is probably the same curious and exciting collection that it has always been: individuals who are both ordinary and extraordinary, gifted and yet vulnerable, strong-willed and motivated people acknowledging the need for a deeper belonging together to sustain and inspire them on the Christian journey. From time to time there is discussion about the paradox that a Community that is so committed to pursuing social justice, to standing alongside those who are marginalised, oppressed and disadvantaged should be made up of people most of whom have had some form of higher education, with few unemployed or living on the poverty line, only four non-white, and a smaller proportion than in previous years even working or living in areas of urban deprivation. Such debates generate a tension that is creative; but the conclusion usually has been that we are not interested in recruitment for its own sake (particularly at a time when there are more applications for membership than the New Members programme can cope with), that we do not seek to be 'representative' either of a cross-section of the wider community or even of the interests that we serve, that we are who we are and should get on with doing what we are called to do, and that our commitment in the pursuit of our concerns will yield its own natural results – 'by their fruits you shall know them'!

Just under half of the Members now (a big swing, this, from earlier days) are in full-time ministry in parishes, chaplaincies (industrial, hospital, and university), theological education, church organisations and the diaconate. Others are drawn from a wide variety of occupations and interests, which often reflect the concerns of the Community. About twenty work in the field of health – as doctors, in nursing, para-medical work and administration, and around the same number are engaged in school and university or college teaching. Others are involved with local government and voluntary organisations, in social and community work and related areas. A number work in industry, some care for families, several are involved in local politics, some are studying and a few are on the staff of the Community. Some are not in paid employment, some work part-time, others share jobs, and several are retired. But all share the commitment to pursue the concerns of the Community and put the Rule into practice in whatever is the most appropriate way in their own situation. This individual commitment to the Rule is the bedrock of the Community's work and whole existence; it is the ultimate embodiment and expression of our vision and understanding of spirituality; and it is in and through this that we seek to support, encourage and challenge one another.

Contrary to what is sometimes suggested, there is really no stereotype of a Community Member: we do not all have beards and wear sandals; we are not all vegetarians, members of the Labour Party, even pacifists; not all the women Members bring their knitting to meetings like tricoteuses at the French Revolution. We are a very motley mixture of old and younger, the ostensibly conventional (indeed four of the six Leaders since the Community was founded were educated at boarding schools and Oxbridge) and the more apparently way-out, of long-distance runners (the Community fielded ninety Members, Associates and other supporters in the 1986 Glasgow Marathon as part of the 'Go 90' campaign to raise money for the MacLeod Centre – the '90' referring to George MacLeod's ninetieth birthday which fell around that time) and of wheelchair-users, of the musically gifted and the tone-deaf. We all have our own stories, many immensely interesting, a variety of spiritual pilgrimages and life-journeys, and we enjoy sharing these – hearing others as much as telling our own! An important and very enriching part of the New Members programme involves listening to one another's stories, the complex of experiences, the development of faith. And one of the most appreciated aspects of Community Week on Iona each year is the series of reports that some Members provide, reflecting on their own situation, their concerns, interests, and work. Inevitably what comes across expresses – both through the formal reports and through all the casual conversations, the accounts of problems, challenges, positive and not so good experiences – a spirituality that has to do with engagement, God's energy at work in so many different ways. While it would obviously be thoroughly invidious to pick out deliberate examples by way of illustration, and there is the added risk that pen-pictures or potted biographies will misrepresent people or do them less than justice, nonetheless I am conscious that one or two illustrations might be helpful at this point. So anonymously, but with their permission, here are summaries of some aspects of the 'stories' of four individuals, drawn not entirely at random, but according to a fixed pattern, from our list of Members.

The first, in her thirties, has been a Member for only a few years but first came into contact with the Community through the annual Greenbelt Festival in Northamptonshire, where the Wild Goose Resource Group, and John Bell in particular, have been participants for some years. Previously she was a teacher in the north of England and now is youth worker in a Church of Scotland parish in Edinburgh. She has also worked as a volunteer and led programme weeks on Iona, is particularly interested in music in worship, and at present convenes the Community's area of concern relating to young people.

The second also lives in Edinburgh now, having moved recently from Kirkcaldy. He is also in his thirties and is a Church of Scotland minister in a lively city-centre congregation. He is married with a young family and his wife is also a Member. He too has a background in youth work and in his previous parish was very involved in the life of the local community, through local politics and in particular through having started an imaginative project to provide support and accommodation for homeless people. He is an avid football fan and travelled to France to watch Scotland in the World Cup. Until just over a year ago he was convener of the Community's islands committee which guides the work of our islands centres.

The third lives at present in the north of England and has had long connections with the Community although she did not become a Member until five years ago. Previously, as a wife and mother, she lived in Africa and London, and in 1996–7 as vice-president of the national Methodist Conference had a very demanding programme of engagements throughout the country over the year. She has a special interest in liturgy and poetry and has worked for the Methodist Church for some time, until recently as editor of a national magazine. She has just left that job with a view to exploring other opportunities.

The fourth has recently retired after ten years or so as the Church of Scotland's Africa Secretary, with responsibilities for links with partner churches and support for missionaries working overseas. After his training for the ministry he worked in Zambia, for some of the time as university chaplain, and on his return to Britain was based in London as Africa Secretary of the British Council of Churches. His experience and knowledge of sub-Saharan Africa, with which the Community has had strong connections for many years, has been immensely helpful to the process of networking and maintaining the Community's involvement in wider political issues.

Dietrich Bonheoffer in *Life Together*, in which he explores the problems, challenges and advantages of living in community, emphasises the significance of a shared discipline; and Walter Brueggemann in *The Prophetic Imagination* draws attention, in the context of the outworking of our corporate and individual vocation, to the significance of the 'concrete discipline of a distinct community'. In the exercise, referred to before, carried out by Peter Millar for the 'rediscovery of spirituality' working group to explore understandings of the concept of spirituality within the Community, one Member said: 'The Community has always resisted having a theological statement to define its position, but it has a discipline and a developing liturgy. These are our distinguishing marks, not statements.'

It is our Rule that holds us together in the Community amid all our diversity. It is no accident that within the New Members programme, within the last review of the Community's 'strategic plan', within the annual reporting letters that Members send to the Leader when they confirm that they are still 'with us' (amusingly, perhaps understandably and unconsciously transmuted into 'with it' by some!), so much attention is given to keeping the Rule. And it is also clear from the correspondence and discussion that takes place when people seek to join the Community that one of the strong attractions is the Rule, the possibility of discipline within highly pressurised lives. It is not that Members and people wanting to join the Community are necessarily disorganised; perhaps a few may be, but the issue for most is about priorities. Many people committed to putting the vision and values of the kingdom into practice tend to be driven workaholics who may well be capable organisers: it is a matter of what one organises oneself to do, in particular whether one leaves enough time for family, leisure and recreation, even sleep. And the particular appeal of the Community's Rule is the mutual accountability: keeping the Rule is not just a matter of personal obedience, between the individual and God, as it were; the idea is that within our local Family Groups we share our experience and account to one another, although inevitably this sounds rather easier in theory than it is in practice – more on this below.

The Rule has evolved over a number of years (and aspects of its development are described in Ralph Morton's *The Iona Community: Personal Impressions of the Early Years*) but has existed more or less in its present form for over thirty years now. It has five parts which complement one another and together represent the integrated approach to spirituality that I am trying to describe and explore throughout this book, motivating us individually and communally through trying to ensure that we are open to and aware of God's energy working in us and through us, thus engaged with God, with one another, with the needs of the world.

There is, first of all, a daily devotional discipline. Members undertake to read the Bible regularly and frequently and to pray for each other, for their shared concerns, and for the wider work of the church on a daily basis. In doing so, alongside other prayer material (for instance publications produced by the various denominations), we use the Community's prayer lectionary and 'directory,' *Miles Christi.* (Difficulties were raised by some pacifist Members, whether because of a lack of a classical education or an extreme literal-mindedness, who objected to the 'soldier of Christ' title, however appropriate it may be as a reflection of our commitment to fight injustice and other evils and as a recollection of George MacLeod's own journey from combat in the first World War to his unshakable and courageous campaigning for nuclear disarmament and non-violence in his later years.) In so doing the whole Community prays each day of the month for common topics and named Members in turn, and the same prayers are included in the morning service in Iona Abbey. Thus for example, on the fifth day of the month (as I write this) we all pray for Members and their partners in one of the Edinburgh Family Groups, for some concerns relating to our mainland work (the Mainland Committee, our magazine *Coracle*, and Columban Houses – the communities of hospitality to be described in Chapter 5), and for the people and countries of the Philippines, Brunei, Malaysia, and Singapore.

It is, of course, one thing to have a devotional discipline; it is much more difficult to keep it! It is clear that many Members struggle and are dissatisfied that they do not, as they see it, manage better. The feelings stem both from practical problems in sustaining a regular pattern in the face of a busy domestic life, a varied work pattern or whatever (easier said than done to get up each day at six o'clock for this purpose, especially if you were very late home for meetings or if you are temperamentally a slow starter in the morning!) and from prayer or Bible reflection seeming empty and arid. The resources recommended in, and the increased discussion and sharing of experience prompted by, the 'tool-kit' recently prepared by the 'rediscovery of spirituality' have been found very helpful here. And it could be argued that the spiritual complacency of feeling pleased with one's achievements would be equally bad, perhaps worse; so perhaps it is better to be struggling but at the same time to be trying to improve the situation and feel that you are getting somewhere.

The second discipline is described as 'sharing and accounting for the use of money'. There is much outside interest in this aspect, partly because money is such a taboo subject in so many circles, especially the Church perhaps – a very private matter, not really respectable to talk about. But we do! This is the element of the Rule where the accountability works best, but even here there is a considerable range of experience, and the difficulties that arise are not to be under-estimated – whether they are problems that arise from dynamics or relationships within the group, or more practical issues about the detailed calculations, for example, what is included and excluded; what account is taken of the situation of an earning partner who is not a Member. Some of these issues are currently being addressed through the production of guidelines and an indication of 'good practice' on the basis of information supplied by the groups on how they go about this task (the extent to which discussion takes place in smaller groups of two, three or four people as against the whole group).

The economic discipline is based on the obligation to account to one another for our use of money. We are encouraged to give away 10 per cent (the traditional tithe) of our personal disposable income, that is, gross income less income tax and other statutory allowances and benefits, together with the cost of agreed 'baseline commitments' and expenses arising from special circumstances – relating, for example, to housing or the support of dependent relatives. This tithe is then divided up so that 6 per cent goes to the wider work of the Church and other charitable purposes (Members' local congregations, bodies concerned with justice and peace, world development, etc.), 2 per cent towards the general work of the Iona Community, 0.5 per cent to particular causes and purposes recommended by Members, with an emphasis on projects in the south world and other areas of special need, 1 per cent for purposes decided by the local Family Group, and 0.5 per cent to a fund to cover travel costs for Members attending plenary meetings.

The third discipline relates to time. It is said that this has its origins in the early days of the Community, when craftsman doubted the ability of ministers to work an eight-hour 'shift'; and there may even be undertones of the assumption, less prevalent nowadays possibly than previously, that only Sundays are to be regarded as ministers' working days! My impression is that Members generally find this the hardest part of the Rule to keep in the face of a combination of a sense of duty that may be over-developed, the culture of the Protestant work-ethic, and a personal tendency towards drivenness. And most Family Groups up until now have not been very effective in fulfilling their responsibility to enable Members to account to one another for the use of time, although there are already encouraging signs that this situation is changing. While some Members, more radically perhaps, express reservations about the discipline itself, on the basis that it views time as a commodity to be measured quantitatively rather than in terms of quality, the wider context in which we live today – with increasingly blurred boundaries between work and leisure as we become a 24-hour, 7-day-a-week society – points towards the value of such a discussion with a view to achieving both balance and creativity. The note in *Miles Christi* says, 'we are all asked to plan our time, in such a way, that proper "weighting" is given, not simply to work, but equally to leisure, to time for family, to developing skills or acquiring new ones, to worship and devotion, to voluntary work – and to sleep!'

Effectively making the bridge between the time discipline and the fourth part of the Rule – the commitment to action for justice and peace in society – Martin Luther King, writing about political engagement from the darkness of a prison cell, said,

> Time itself is neutral; it can be used either destructively or constructively. More and more I feel that the people of ill will have used time much more effectively than have people of good will. We have to repent in this generation not merely for the hateful word and actions of the bad people, but for the appalling silence of the good people. Human progress never rolls in on wheels of inevitability; it comes through the tireless efforts of women and men willing to be co-workers with God, and without this hard work, time itself becomes the ally of the forces of social stagnation. We must use time creatively, in the knowledge that the time is always ripe to do the right.

In one sense this is the most recent part of the Rule, since in this form it dates only from 1988, but it is an extension, incorporating a wider range of themes and references relating to justice as well as peace, of the earlier communal Peace Commitment agreed in 1966. It is this commitment that in many people's eyes gives the Community its distinctiveness, in not just believing that peace and justice are 'good things' but being prepared, within a framework of mutual accountability, to do something about it. And, alongside the other elements of the Rule, it takes Members' commitment out into the world, gives it shape and direction, and in so doing embodies and articulates the spirituality of engagement.

The final part of the five-fold Rule is the fundamental commitment to meet with and account to one another. Four times a year there are plenary meetings, as described in more detail elsewhere, three times, at weekends, on the mainland and Community Week on Iona in the summer. Most Members, other than the few based overseas, manage to attend at least one or two of the mainland plenaries each year, at which the average attendance is around 80, and over recent years 120 or so, along with their families, have come to Community Week. The venues of the mainland plenaries shift around: the annual general meeting is always in Glasgow in the early summer, but the October and February meetings were held in Stirling (on peace issues) and Manchester (the 'new economics') in 1996, in Lanarkshire (violence against women) and Crieff (St Ninian and St Columba) in 1997, at Dunblane (the possibility of a new mainland base for the Community) and Newcastle (work with young people) in 1998, and will go to Stirling (the World Council of Churches Harare theme – 'Turn to God: rejoice in hope') and Edinburgh in 1999 (a perspective on the millennium, including the inter-faith dimension).

An important aspect of Members' meeting together involves the readiness to take part in the working groups and committees which provide advice and decide on the Community's work, but for most people the main place of belonging together, where the spirituality is rooted, is in the local Family Groups. This is where the mutual accounting takes place, where Members share news and concerns, where there are opportunities to discuss issues of common interest, whether of local significance or relating to policy directions in the life of the wider Community. There are at present twenty-six Family Groups throughout Britain, seventeen in Scotland and nine in England, but beyond that the structure is scarcely uniform: the size varies depending on where Members live, but the optimum size is reckoned to be about fourteen; some groups, for instance in the west Highlands or in East Anglia and south-west England, cover large areas while there are five groups in Edinburgh and four in and around Glasgow; most groups meet monthly but some meet at weekends, most in the evening but at least one in daytime during the week, according to Members' convenience and circumstances; some groups include a few Associate Members, where there is space and a commitment to attend regularly (although this sometimes raises complications for the process of Members' accounting); some Members' partners attend, even if they are not Associates, others do not.

Similarly there are variations in what happens when a group meets. All will include, at or near the start of proceedings, the Community's 'office', the short act of worship that is printed in *Miles Christi*, the elements of which correspond to part of the daily morning service in Iona Abbey. Thereafter there is likely to be a sharing of news and concerns, and some groups at some of their meetings may not go beyond this – because sometimes there may be much to share, personal, social and political. Then there may be the main item for discussion, whether accounting for some aspect of the Rule, a paper on a matter of Community policy referred to Family Groups for views, an issue of wider concern, or whatever. Many groups celebrate Communion together, some at the end of each meeting, some less frequently. And for almost every group an important part of the belonging together is the shared hospitality, whether the kind of 'pot luck' meal that some groups have, the informal discussion over coffee and biscuits or wine and cheese, or the annual Christmas parties and summer picnics that many arrange.

Clearly for the groups to function properly, as a means of both challenge and support to Members, and for them to fulfil their intention in terms of the process of mutual accounting, there must be a high degree of trust among the members of the group. Sometimes this is hard to achieve in situations where the composition of a group is perpetually changing, as tends to happen with the city groups especially. But lack of change within a group can equally be a problem, where a group may, however unconsciously, have developed a settled way of co-existing harmoniously that may avoid some of the hard questions that accounting demands; in this case the infusion of new blood can be helpful in rediscovering the cutting edge of challenge, and where Members bring experience of another group they have belonged to elsewhere, or where a new Member is prepared, difficult as it can be, to rock the boat a bit by sharing some of the insights and sense of vision that the New Members programme can develop this can be very beneficial.

Largely as a result of such variations there is an inevitable unevenness in how Family Groups approach the process of mutual accounting. For some it is the whole rationale of the group's existence and flows through all the meetings, emerging at some points more explicitly – where, for example, the details involved in the economic discipline are addressed and examined. For others it will figure at points throughout the annual programme, although clearly if a group meets monthly and deals fully with each of the elements of the Rule at one or more meetings there may not be much time to pursue other concerns throughout the year.

Recognition of the fundamental importance of Family Groups to the life, vision and corporate spirituality of the Community has from time to time prompted consideration of the possibility of getting all the Family Group conveners together with a view to sharing experience and ideas, but the practical problems involved in assembling twenty-six busy people from all over Britain has so far prevented this happening; even a meeting during Community Week, when a high proportion of the conveners are likely to be present, has not happened because of the pressures of time during the week. But the spirituality 'tool-kit', already mentioned, contains suggestions for a 'Family Group' audit, enabling and encouraging the group to examine and appraise its own process and purpose, and it is clear that the use of this has enhanced and deepened the life of most of the groups that have used it.

Clearly the Leader of the Community has a particular function in relation to the Membership and the functioning of the Rule. In fact the very title, however appropriate it may have been to the time and style of George MacLeod during his term (1938–67), has really been something of a misnomer ever since. The Leader's job as it has evolved is really to hold it all together, a task, as has been said of others, that demands the judgment of Solomon and the patience of Job. With the growth of the organisation the administrative aspects, both paperwork and staff and financial management, have grown, but, just as Ralph Morton was of immense assistance to George MacLeod, so over the last twenty years or so, the appointment of deputy leaders and now of a support services manager, has lightened the load in this respect. The Leader is thus both the chief executive of a medium-sized voluntary organisation and the Community's official representative to the outside world – to the Church, the media and all those who write, phone and want someone to come and speak to them about the Community's work and concerns.

Through the involvement of both staff and Members in dealing with this aspect of the work, the Leader can devote attention to the other parts of the job which relate to the Community as movement rather than organisation – the pastoral aspect, involving the keeping of contact and providing support and encouragement; the liturgical, both during time on Iona and responding to invitations to preach or conduct worship at specific events and gatherings; above all the maintenance and development of the Community's vision and direction, an amorphous process of nurturing, testing and discernment that involves much discussion, floating and exchange of reflections and ideas. Since George MacLeod's time, the Leader has had a seven-year term of office, and uniquely within the Community the post of Leader is filled by election: one does not apply for such a life-changing experience!

As others have discovered before me, being Leader of the

Iona Community is a way of life rather than just a job; it is immensely exciting, challenging, stretching and rewarding; it is like a juggling act, keeping plates spinning or a lot of balls in the air at once; and it is an awesome and formidable task to be the person, to whom, for a few years, the torch has been passed, the responsibility for looking after this very precious and rather fragile Community. It is a great relief – and here is where our understanding of spirituality surfaces again – that I do not do so alone but am supported and surrounded by the 'great cloud of witnesses' and by the love, prayers, good wishes and practical help of so many people both within the Community's official 'constituency' and outside.

In closing this chapter about the membership and the Rule, it is important to keep in mind the significance of this wider constituency to our continuing work. They share our vision and our commitment in so many ways, undergirded by their sympathy with our understanding and approach to spirituality. Scarcely a year passes without a few Members leaving: once a month we remember those of our membership who have died; people's circumstances change so that, for reasons like distance or other commitments, they find it hard to sustain the requirements of the Rule, and we want membership, while inevitably demanding to be ultimately helpful and enriching, not an intolerable burden or a cause of guilt. Only a few have left in recent years because of any major dispute or difference of view over priorities or direction.

And almost all who resign as Members remain part of the formal 'family' as Associate Members or Friends. It is a great encouragement that at present the numbers of Associate Members, as with the Members, seem to be rising each year, as people are attracted by our work, whether after time spent on Iona or through contact elsewhere with our work and concerns. Associates are invited to renew their commitment annually on St Columba's Day (9 June), have their own Rule (involving the same devotional discipline as Members and the opportunity to share in a corporate economic witness), receive regular copies of *Coracle*, and are encouraged to visit Iona when possible. In addition to a degree of participation by Associates in Members' Family Groups, as mentioned above, there is a network of Associates groups (or, more correctly, 'Iona groups') throughout Britain, locally initiated and organised, providing opportunities for people to share common concerns and develop their interest and understanding in the field of spirituality and social witness. This network is co-ordinated through the Associates Advisory Group which meets annually, a very useful occasion for co-ordination, communication and generation of energy and encouragement, and comprises over twenty 'regional representatives' covering the whole of Britain.

Of course not all Associates wish or have sufficient free time to attend meetings regularly. To an even greater extent than with the Members, to whose commitment the Rule gives a common shape, there is variety and flexibility – an openness and provisionality – that may be Spirit-inspired or simply born of reluctance to impose more structure than seems necessary, but which somehow feels appropriate both to our understanding of spirituality and to our wish to leave scope for people to involve themselves in and identify themselves with the life of the Community in whatever way and to whatever extent they wish and can. We are continually grateful and immensely encouraged that so many choose to do so; and in the mystery and wonder of our pilgrimage together it is always helpful to be reminded, in the words of Jean Vanier, founder of L'Arche Community, what our belonging together is ultimately all about:

> Community life is there to help us not to flee from our deep wound, but to remain with the reality of love. It is there to help us believe that our illusions and egoism will be gradually healed if we become nourishment for others.

We are in community for each other, so that all of us can grow and uncover our wound before the infinite, so that Jesus can manifest himself through it. (Jean Vanier, *The Broken Body*)

Help us all to discipline ourselves,
assessing how we fall short,
giving account to each other of our faith,
our prayer,
and how we live our lives,
that when people ask about the Kingdom of God
we can point to the quality of our life together.
('*Pray Now*', Church of Scotland)

O Christ, the Master Carpenter, who at the last through wood and nails purchased our whole salvation, wield well your tools in the workshop of your world, that we who come rough-hewn to your bench may here be fashioned to a truer beauty of your hand. We ask it for your own name's sake. Amen (From the 'Office' of the Iona Community)

5

The Iona Experience

One of the guests at the Iona Community's MacLeod Centre was bidding farewell to the group of people with whom she had spent the week, exploring issues of identity and belonging through art and craft. As is the case almost every week they were gathered from a variety of social and denominational backgrounds and from different parts of the world – individuals and couples from Germany, Australia, America, England and Scotland, together with an amazing extended family who lived together in a former convent in Essex, a woman with her sister and over thirty of the fifty or so children she had fostered over the years, many with special needs and some now with their own families. It had been a typical Iona experience, rather sticky to start with, as strangers got to know one another, thrust together in this place that was unfamiliar to most of them, building relationships through discussions at meal times, over chores, in programme sessions, at social events or walks to the beach; but by the time Thursday came the group was well integrated and now this woman had to go, rather earlier than the rest, because she was going on to the second part of her holiday in Spain, and she blamed 'the Scottish transport' for having to leave so early to catch her flight. In fact, coming from where she did in the Midlands, the same problem would have arisen if she had been, for instance, on the Scilly Isles: it was not because she was in Scotland so much as in a relatively remote location that the logistical difficulty occurred and travelling took so long. It is very much quicker to go to the south of France, Italy or Greece than it is to travel to Iona – from the central belt of Scotland cities as well as from England. Even from Glasgow it is a journey of around six hours by public transport, and without a car from the other main centres of population in Scotland it is necessary to come through Glasgow. It is remarkable, and immensely encouraging to the Iona Community, how many people make the long journey, often involving overnight stops *en route*, or in the case of exceptionally dedicated and intrepid souls driving through the night, to come to the Community's centres on Iona. But for many the remoteness is part of the attraction and the journey part of the experience.

In the Middle Ages, however, Iona stood not so much 'on the edge' of things but, in days before the development of overland transportation when communication by sea was the primary mode, rather at the crossroads. There is a very interesting variety of accounts of the reasons and circumstances of the coming of Columba to Iona in 563. Ian Bradley's *Columba, Pilgrim and Penitent*, mentioned earlier, explores the historical background in the light of the most recent scholarship and gives an excellent account of the life and significance of Columba and the monastery he founded, and its claims to recognition as the cradle of Christianity in Scotland (although hardly 'the birthplace of Christianity', as one of the recent tourist posters suggested!).

As the histories of Iona tell the Columban monastery flourished as an influential centre of mission, hospitality and artistic endeavour until, around the end of the ninth century, following a series of Viking raids in which many of the monks were killed, most of those left returned to Ireland. Three centuries later Reginald, Lord of the Isles, invited the Benedictine order to Iona and, on the site of the original Celtic settlement, the Abbey was built and extended, as the work developed over the years, with a more devotional, less outgoing emphasis than the missionary Columban monks, until following the Reformation in the second half of the sixteenth century it ceased to function and gradually fell into disrepair. The popularity of Iona as a place of pilgrimage grew down the centuries – with the interest of the graves of Kings of Scotland, Norway and France in the burial-ground (called Reilig Odhrain, after the first of the Columban monks to die) alongside the historic ruins of the Benedictine monastery and of the Augustinian nunnery, which had existed at the same time but, like most Scottish nunneries, has little recorded history.

Now looking both back and forward at the end of the twentieth century, one can see several different movements in play, both restoration and expansion on the one hand, and decline on the other; and it is a considerable challenge, whether to the Iona Community or to anyone else, to discern, with spiritual insight and balanced judgment, what is happening, where God's purpose is leading, what, as it were, the signs of the times are telling us. It is not only in the Community's islands centres that there has been experience of increasing scale and pace, rebuilding and building. More and more visitors are coming to Iona, as many as sixteen hundred in a single day sometimes, it is reckoned, with up to eighteen coaches parked at Fionnphort, some on the regular trips of the local Mull bus companies, others from as far afield as Germany and Italy, including Iona in their tour of Scotland. To cater for this traffic, and for the holiday trade, the hotels and the local restaurant/pub have all expanded and increased bed-and-breakfast accommodation is available, although because of the protected conservation status of the island there has been little new building – only a few houses, all for people already living and working on Iona. But there are also striking trends in the opposite direction. In the early nineteenth century over 500 people lived on Iona, but, owing principally to economic pressures by the turn of the century the population had dropped to 213 and at the last official census in 1991 stood at 130. Now despite the influx of visitors there is considerable local concern about the future of the island with few young families (only four children at the school) and discussion of a potentially controversial proposal to improve communication with Mull by building a 'fixed-link', with possible economic and social benefits, across the Sound of Iona.

In the face of all these fluctuations, pressures and uncertainties, the theme of trust seems fundamental – both because, in an increasingly demanding situation, it is necessary to trust in God and develop a genuine trust in one another, founded on open, honest relationships; and because of the interest that several formal Trusts have had and still have in Iona itself. The eighth Duke of Argyll, as the local landowner, transferred the historic buildings (for which a programme of consolidation had already been started) to the Iona Cathedral Trustees, who, following a major public appeal in 1979, established a management company (Iona Abbey Ltd) to exercise their day-to-day responsibilities for the external fabric of the buildings generally and for the interior also of the Abbey church. To carry out this work Iona Abbey Ltd employ a squad of skilled workmen and, in addition to public grants (for example from Historic Scotland, the European Commission, and the National Lottery Heritage Fund) for particular projects, depend on donations which visitors are invited to contribute as they enter the Abbey grounds. The Iona Community is responsible for internal maintenance of the buildings it occupies under the terms agreed with the Trustees, but in effect as custodian of the buildings, including the church, over the period since the Community was founded, itself shows a high level of commitment and dedication to the buildings, not only in their use for daily worship but also through the provision of guiding services and regular cleaning. Indeed there is no doubt that the considerable attraction of the buildings, and the fact that the number of visitors to Iona remains steady or even rises at a time when tourism in the area and in Scotland generally may be going through hard times, is due to the presence of a vibrant living, worshipping and welcoming community with a world-wide vision and concern that is rooted in the spirituality of engagement which is the theme of this book.

The island of Iona itself was sold by the Trustees of the tenth Duke of Argyll to the Fraser Foundation, who presented it to the Scottish nation in memory of Lord Fraser of Allander, and ownership was transferred to the National Trust for Scotland, who thus are key players, along with the local authority (Argyll and Bute Council) and the local community council, in decisions about the island's future. Few visitors to Iona will be aware of the subtleties of the relationships and precise allocation of responsibilities among the various bodies involved. However, for the future well-being of all concerned with Iona, local people and the Iona Community alike, together with the various other bodies mentioned, it is very clear that there must be a fuller recognition of the others' interests, of the need for open communication and discussion and the common advantage there is in harmonious, co-operative relationship.

This is the context within which the Iona Community seeks to carry out its work on Iona, offering to visitors hospitality and the attractive services of the Abbey shop and the coffee house, providing opportunities for staff and guests to share the common life, seeking to embody the integrated approach to spirituality, energising and engaged, that this book is exploring. Ron Ferguson, in the preface to his biography of George MacLeod, expresses the purpose of the Community generally in a way that is true also in relation to the particular work of the islands centres: 'The Iona Community sees its primary task as being the discovery and making of community in a world divided; making peace in the midst of violence, discovering dignified and justly-rewarded work for all; witnessing to the power of God and the worth of each other.'

Many people come to the Community's islands centres with particular expectations, based no doubt on what they may have previously heard or read about Iona or the Community. Some will have heard of Iona through their contact with the Wild Goose Resource Group or with some of the songs or other liturgical material produced by them; they may be surprised, even disappointed, to find that the members of the Group are not based on Iona and that the worship in the Abbey church draws on a whole range of material within the tradition of the Church. There is also the assumption, referred to and corrected in a previous chapter, that what happens on Iona represents the sum total of the Iona Community's activities – although, in the light of the depth and intensity of the experience that people often have, when you are on Iona it is all too easy for it to feel like the centre of the universe, and nothing else seems to matter much.

Or, again, there may be an expectation that it is some kind of therapeutic community so that people's personal, pastoral needs will be ministered to with skill and sensitivity. This is a difficult issue, which both in a sense touches the heart of the Community's understanding of spirituality, and relates to the Community's approach to the ministry of healing, of which more will be said later. We believe that each one of us is less than whole and therefore in need of healing. But we also believe that, reflecting the idea of spirituality as connectedness, the process through which God's healing power works is a corporate one. So there is no attempt through the work of the islands centres to offer a deliberate pastoral ministry to people with special needs; there is no member of staff appointed to be 'chaplain' or 'pastoral counsellor', no one whose job description includes responsibilities in this field. Nonetheless it is inevitable that, as in any other situation where people gather, pastoral needs arise, and they will be dealt with in a number of ways – in the case of staff, through a variety of established support systems and management processes; in the case of a guest, through the availability of a sympathetic and understanding response, often within from among the guests themselves, or if the situation requires specialist skill by reference to professional facilities.

Other people – and this tends to be true of both guests and staff (who do not read too carefully the material they receive beforehand!) – may be looking for a particular kind of spiritual experience: space and time for reflection, perhaps even a spiritual director available to give them guidance. They discover something rather different for, 'in the memorable words of a member of staff on Iona, "People come to us seeking peace and quiet and we try to send them away seeking peace and justice".' (Association of Laity Centres newsletter – spring 1998)

I explored this very theme – the Iona experience, expectation and reality, also reflecting again the theology and spirituality of the Community – in a sermon in Iona Abbey in July 1997:

> So often Iona is perceived as a place of peace and tranquillity. And of course, despite the frequent crowds of visitors between the jetty and Abbey, many of us do discover this kind of peace here. I had a strong sense of it the other day walking back home towards the machair on a clear still night; in the half-darkness I could just see a tiny frog jumping across the path to keep out of my way; the croak of the corncrake penetrated the silence. And the next morning it was dry, calm and warm for the first time in the week as I went for my daily jog across the machair to Port Ban. It was so peaceful until I encroached on the territory of the oyster-catchers at the far end of the

> Bay at the Back of the Ocean: they shrieked at me angrily, perhaps protecting a nest, and I thought for a moment they were going to dive-bomb me rather like terns do. In one sense it was anything but peaceful; in another sense there was harmony, mutual respect, a balance of right relationships. Real peace, deep peace does have a disturbing cutting edge; it is not just a frothy, feel-good, be-nice-to-everybody business. When in our Iona morning service, we say, 'We will seek peace and pursue it', we also say, 'We will not offer to God offerings that cost us nothing'. The peace that many people find here turns out to be very different from what they expected – not the rather sanitised 'God's in his heaven, all's right with the world' variety; more challenging and engaged than that. Along with the conviction that 'all shall be well, and all manner of thing shall be well'[as Julian of Norwich put it], there is a surprising restlessness, a desire to move and change, the realisation that in our pursuit of God's peace it is our vocation to play a part in the process of resistance to all in today's culture and society that obstructs the fulfilment of God's purpose and the coming of the Kingdom.

In *Chasing the Wild Goose* Ron Ferguson describes how

> the inspiration of what happens on Iona has been constant, amidst the ups and downs and struggles of the Iona Community's life . . . People who arrived at the jetty on Iona tired and depressed very often left a week later changed and invigorated, ready to face again the challenge of living a Christian witness in the situation from which they had come.

It is something of a mystery, a miracle of grace that is hard to understand, explain, and even describe. Essentially the Iona experience for many people is one of transformation, of exploring broader horizons, discerning new possibilities, seeing fresh connections between faith and life, discovering, by living it, the significance of an integrated approach to spirituality of engagement, deepening Christian commitment by coming closer to God and to one another in work and worship. This is what is involved in the opportunity to 'share the common life' that is offered in our three islands centres where there is a common rhythm, although the weekly programmes in each may have differences of emphasis. It is an experience involving grace and generosity, vulnerability and hospitality, in the course of which minds are challenged and hearts are touched, where there may well be both laughter and tears, where risks may be taken and insights gained both into the nature and purpose of God and into what God is calling us to do and be. It is an experience that relates to basic issues of identity, belonging, values and priorities and that recognises the spiritual reality that individual fulfilment is to be discovered only in community, that self-development cannot be achieved apart from a concern for one another and for the world around us, that all this is embraced and caught up in our relationship with God.

All our literature and publicity material, not least the programmes for our islands centres each year, makes it very clear that what the Community offers on Iona is neither the conventional kind of retreat nor a conference centre in the usual sense. In particular there are the expectation that guests will share in the domestic chores, and there are multi-bedded rooms in all our centres; at a time when so many people in going on holiday or to events at other church centres are looking for single rooms and *en suite* facilities, it is encouraging that the demand for places at our centres on Iona remains so high – especially since financial and architectural considerations, as well as a commitment to simplicity of life-style, in any case rule out that possibility!

Whatever the reasons for people's coming to our islands centres, whatever their expectations, realisable or not, precious as the work and particular location on Iona is, the Community has the sense of sharing also in a project on a wider scale and seeks also to convey this to all who come: this has to do not only with the links with the wider work of the Community itself, or indeed with the Church at national or world level, important as these are; it relates also to providence, the purposes and promises of God. So just as Columba, in a very moving and attractive prayer attributed to him (and included at the end of this chapter) conveyed a strong awareness of his shortcomings and relative insignificance within the divine scheme of things, so too the Iona Community is conscious of our 'faults and failings' (which we remember in our communal prayer of confession). We certainly do not pretend to get everything right (both because we are human and therefore flawed and because to explore and experiment involves the risk of making mistakes) and we recognise that what we do stands alongside the work and concerns of all others who are impelled by the vision and values of the kingdom and sustained by the grace of God.

This too is an important part of 'the Iona experience' and usually evokes a positive response among many of the people who come to Iona and appreciate the wider perspective that is involved in sharing in the life at our islands centres, experiencing new, more inclusive, participative ways that make worship come alive, and seeking to relate the Christian faith more relevantly to the issues of today. Many of those who come do so often because they feel disappointed with what they perceive as the static narrowness of much of mainstream church life or because they are disillusioned with the prevailing culture of acquisitive individualism and are looking for something more substantial, something perhaps that is worth setting their sights on, even staking their lives on. Our hope is that, in however small a way, in the Iona experience their lives may be touched and transfigured by the risen Christ, that they may glimpse afresh the promises and purposes of God, surprising, energising, challenging. In so doing we see ourselves sharing in the legacy of Columba, in the pilgrimage towards tomorrow that is the missionary priority for today.

The life and rhythm of the Community's islands centres is rooted in the Community's understanding of spirituality – the integration and balance of the different components of the daily programme, the interaction among staff and guests, the engagement with people and issues, the commitment to process, the purposeful progression through the week, the sense of journeying on to further reflection and with strengthened commitment. The significance of community life is fundamental. There is a continuing resident community of staff, some on three-year contracts dealing with particular areas (the Warden, and the Director of the MacLeod Centre, those responsible, for example, for programme, staff and maintenance co-ordination, supervision of domestic arrangements, office management) and others come for a shorter period of around a year to work in posts such as cook, housekeeper, musician, craft worker. There is also a wider staff community comprising resident staff along with volunteers, drawn from a rich diversity of ages and nationalities, who come for shorter periods of between six weeks and three months – students and unemployed people, some who are retired, on unpaid or sabbatical leave, even on holiday.

This is an ever-changing community as volunteers come and go during the season; through experience and discussion it works out its own routines for co-operation and sharing and has its own internal regular processes for support and reflection, alongside the arrangements for relating the life and work of the centres to the wider Membership and Community structures. The 'Iona experience' for many staff is intense and deep, even life-changing; strong friendships may be formed, religious convictions deepened, self-confidence boosted as individuals are valued and listened to and untapped skills are discovered and released. But the pressures of the work can be unrelenting and time-off is important. A rigorous approach to job responsibilities or contracted hours is impossible in circumstances where flexibility and helping one another out is often necessary, and ways have to be found of amicable co-existence through differences and conflicts of personality in a living and working situation from which one cannot readily escape!

But the basic community on Iona, the *raison d'être* as it were, is the community of staff and guests which forms and re-forms each week; and the emotional effect upon the staff of the regular cycle of welcomes and farewells, and the ebb and flow of relationships is not to be underestimated. The most difficult, but also the best weeks on Iona tend to be those where people come together from a diversity of backgrounds – where there is an 'open week', say, at the MacLeod Centre involving a group from a middle-class Anglican parish in the south of England along with a school group from a housing scheme in one of Scotland's cities; or when individual guests from all over Britain and beyond gather for a week at the Abbey to explore some theme relating to the concerns of the Community, from racism to ecology, from human sexuality to non-violence. The tag associated with the ecumenical movement in Britain – 'not strangers but pilgrims' – could well be applied to the Iona experience: there may be an initial shyness and awkwardness, but after a week's sharing the common life there is such a sense both of being valued as an individual and of belonging together that many are reluctant to leave.

The activities each week, and each day within each week, follow a regular pattern that is integrated and well-tested. Worship and work, meals and social events flow into one another in a way that was characteristic also of the Celtic and Benedictine traditions practised on Iona in yesteryears. After breakfast the morning worship in the Abbey church (except on Sunday when there is a Communion service along fairly traditional lines, with the church full to overflowing in the summer months) uses a fixed liturgy, with scope within it for minor variations. The guests then go to do daily chores in their centres. During the morning there are usually programme sessions around the theme of the week, discussions, workshops, creative opportunities through craft and music. After lunch there is often free time for guests to explore the island together, to visit the nearby island of Staffa, famous for its puffins and Fingal's cave, and sometimes extra sessions – for example, worship planning, singing. After the evening meal there is another session – introductory at the beginning of the week, evaluating and reflecting on the week at its end; and a regular talk and discussion about the Iona Community one night, and on others the Community's peace and justice commitment, and its approach to the ministry of healing. While clearly the whole week has a social dimension, with plenty of opportunity for informal conversations at meal-times and on other occasions, there are two special events – a ceilidh in the village hall after the evening service on Tuesday, when others on the island also are able to join in the singing and Scottish dancing; and a concert on Thursday planned and performed by guests in the centres, usually involving a combination of 'party-pieces' and humorous songs or sketches composed in the light of the week's experience. The evening services follow a different theme each day – welcome on Saturday, quiet time on Sunday, justice and peace (usually focusing on a specific topic or concern) on Monday, prayers for healing on Tuesday, a service planned and led by guests in one of the centres on Wednesday, an opportunity on Thursday for people to make or renew a commitment to follow in the way of Jesus, and on Friday an informal Communion both rounding off the week's experience and sending them out on the next stage of their journeys.

The programme at Camas follows different lines entirely,

reflecting the different scale and setting, and the different groups, often with a range of special needs, using the centre, so that there is an emphasis on outdoor adventure activities and on issues relating to the environment, with a greater degree of interaction generally between the staff and guests. Moreover, the remoteness and closeness to sea and land, together with the lack of electricity and flush toilets, add another distinctive and attractive dimension. The general impact of the experience, however, and the extent to which this reflects and impinges upon the Community's approach to spirituality, is very similar to the experience on Iona. Camas occupies a special place in the hearts and minds of many Community Members, largely because of the very rich experiences they have had there during the annual New Members' work week in the summer. As part of an exercise in the Community's considering the future of its islands work, a business plan was recently prepared specifically for Camas. It summed up the experience of Camas very effectively and succinctly:

> It is understood that the spiritual life of all who experience Camas is nourished not only by the daily times of reflection, but by the whole experience of living in community together. The development of an ecological dimension in the life and work of Camas, along with greater awareness of the geography and history of the place, and an increased use of artistic expression, has led to the development of a holistic and integrated community, where care for oneself, for others, and for the environment are different aspects of a shared experience. With its simple, down-to-earth life-style, closeness to nature, smallness of scale and spiritual values, Camas is a place which is at the same time safe and yet challenging, supportive and yet offering the possibility for creativity, self-discovery and social responsibility. Thousands of young people have found it a place of peace and adventure,

which, though remote, opens up new possibilities and a network of global connections, as horizons are expanded.

One of the Community's familiar prayers, quoted in full at the end of the previous chapter, talks of Iona, and its Abbey in particular, being 'a sanctuary and a light'. This is the essence of the Iona experience: it is a place where, at its best, and in the usual course of things, there is a supportive environment and a sense of being surrounded and sustained by the love of God so that people can feel safe despite all life's uncertainties – to love and be welcomed, loved and valued for oneself, to share vulnerability and anxieties, to reflect and explore. And since our journeys go beyond Iona it may not always be quite so safe because the reflections may be challenging and disturbing! The light may reveal new possibilities and new directions, just as the light in Iona Abbey comes from sometimes surprising places. One of George MacLeod's familiar prayers, much used especially in the early days of the Community, was 'Pray for more light and follow the light you have.'

In ways that are mysterious and miraculous, surprising and wonderful, so many people's lives are illuminated and energised, touched and transformed by the light and love which come from God, their faith reawakened and deepened by their time on Iona, connected in new ways with contemporary concerns through the strong sense of being held along with others in the Creator's hand. It is a truly healing experience. For centuries people have come to Iona seeking healing and the Iona Community's commitment to the ministry of healing is a natural corollary of its approach to spirituality. This is a dimension of ministry that has become marginal to the mainstream life of the Church, although there are signs of increasing numbers of congregations including healing prayers regularly in their services. The Community seeks to follow Jesus's command to be a healing church and his own healing ministry of which the Gospel accounts are full. We look not necessarily for bodily healing or 'miracle cures' but express through the various parts of this ministry the mutual support and healing which our world needs and we all need as individuals on our journey through life, rough or smooth. Christ's healing touch of divine love and forgiveness reached into the deepest places of people's lives and affected different levels of mind and body. Healing is about wholeness, connectedness, the integration and fulfilment of personhood that is God's purpose for us and fundamental to our spirituality. A recent – September 1998 – edition of the American Episcopal journal *The Witness* referred to 'the spiritual insight that beyond the broken surface of our lives there is a "hidden wholeness" on which all life depends . . . this we seek through all our years; to be complete and of one piece, within, without'.

From Iona a circle of intercessory prayer, reaching out throughout Britain and beyond, is co-ordinated by a member of the resident staff, remembering the needs of people for whom prayers have been specially requested. It is perhaps important to note that through intercessory prayer there is no question of seeking to change God, but rather to share with Jesus Christ in the vital work of redeeming and transforming the world and to open up the possibility that through us God's healing energy may be released and experienced in situations of darkness and despair. This sense of 'a ceaseless chain of prayer' is evident too in the creation of a quiet and beautiful place of prayer in the south aisle of the Abbey church, where candles lit by guests and visitors in prayer for people and places are always burning, and it also runs through the Tuesday evening service in the Abbey church each week, when prayers are offered, as requested, for particular places and situations, and the laying on of hands is offered, not by any specific 'gifted' individual but as a corporate act of as many as wish to take part, under the leadership each week of different members of the resident staff group. The healing ministry is thus affirmed as an inclusive process, complementary, it must be stressed, to the medical services through which God's healing power is working. It is a process in which we all express our need for support and our obedience to the command to go forth and heal, in which we pray for situations as well as individuals that need healing, in which we recognise that in healing each of us has much to give and receive as we all grow towards the wholeness that is God's purpose of renewal, transfiguration and liberation for the world.

For many people the high point of the Iona experience is the 'Pilgrimage' round the island that takes place every Wednesday. Within the tradition of the Church down the centuries pilgrimage is an outward sign of the inner journey towards God – the search for meaning, inspiration, healing and redirection mirroring the deeply personal desire for forgiveness and renewal. The Iona pilgrimage is open to holiday-makers and visitors as well as the guests at the Community's centres and provides a marvellous chance for conversation and discussion. It is a guided walk led by members of the resident staff group, a peripatetic act of worship, covering about seven miles and taking up to six hours, stopping for a prayer, song and brief meditation at places of historic and religious significance, reflecting on the journey of our own lives and the life of the world. And in so doing it sums up, within the compass of a single event, the Iona experience and the Community's understanding of spirituality.

The pilgrimage starts at St Martin's Cross outside the west door of the Abbey. The cross, with its typical Celtic interwoven design, is well over a thousand years old and is dedicated to the memory of St Martin of Tours, fourth-century warrior turned peace-maker (like George MacLeod many centuries later) who was one of the pioneers of monasticism and whose mission influenced the development of the Celtic Church. High crosses like this were gathering-points for open-air worship within the Celtic tradition and the characteristically encircled cross proclaims the meeting of heaven and earth in the Gospel that touches every aspect of the world's life.

The next stop is the Augustinian nunnery, which, as mentioned earlier, dates from the same period as the Benedictine monastery and has a beautiful garden among the ruins. The nunnery has had little historical attention down the years, a clear reflection of the subordination of women in both church and society for centuries. Here there is an opportunity to consider how there was a greater balance between the feminine and masculine within the Celtic Church and the extent to which groups within society today are still discriminated against and disempowered.

The Pilgrimage then leaves the village and heads towards the west side of the island, stopping on the machair (Gaelic for 'small plain', usually by the sea, or sometimes 'raised beach'), now used by the farmers for common grazing, also the island's golf course naturally maintained, in earlier centuries the cornfield for both Celtic and Benedictine monasteries. So in a world of competition the machair, where, at the beautiful Bay at the Back of the Ocean close to the famous Spouting Cave, the Pilgrimage stops later for lunch on its way back, is like a parable of co-operation and sharing in a world where so many are still poor and hungry.

Just after leaving the machair there is a pause at Loch Staonaig, formerly the island's reservoir. Now, under European regulations, the islands water comes from Mull and Loch Staonaig is used only in emergencies. Here we reflect on our dependence on water and on how we take its availability for granted; a contrast to some African countries, for example, where women walk for many miles to fetch water to keep their families alive.

Then the Pilgrimage proceeds across moorland, bog and heather, after a steep descent, to the Marble Quarry in a little inlet, that may be a little hard for the uninitiated to find, on the south-east side of the island. Here are the remains of the machinery, now preserved by the National Trust as industrial architecture, which was used to quarry the very distinctive serpentine-streaked marble around the turn of the century – including the Benedictines' altar from a much earlier period of working and the magnificent Communion table that now stands in the Abbey church. Here too are some of the oldest stones in the world (Lewisian gneiss which has been here for almost three thousand million years). Erik Cramb, a Community Member who is now an industrial chaplain based in Dundee and co-ordinator of Scottish Churches Industrial Mission, recalls hearing here

> George MacLeod at his eloquent best about the rock, so ancient, being like Nelson's Column in age, Old Testament times the thickness of a matchbox and New Testament times the thickness of a stamp. But I remember being distracted by the rusting remains of the marble cutting machinery whose working life in the quarry had been so brief and the rock so seemingly eternal. There's a spirituality in the stones and the rust speaking – shouting aloud.

Here on the Pilgrimage it is customary to give thanks for the goodness of creation and seek forgiveness where natural resources have been exploited and not used with care and responsibility.

The Pilgrimage then heads for St Columba's Bay, the Port of the Coracle where Columba and his followers are supposed to have landed in 563 after their momentous journey from Ireland. The nearby hill is called the Cairn of the Back to Ireland where it was ascertained that Ireland could not be seen from Iona. Here people are invited to think about new beginnings, and by tradition to throw a pebble into the sea, representing something they want to be rid of and leave behind.

After lunch on the machair there is a long walk to the Hermit's Cell, situated in an isolated spot in the middle of the island, not far from but out of sight of the monastic buildings. This circle of stones is, according to tradition but without archaeological support, taken to be the remains of a Celtic beehive hut where monks may have spent periods in solitude and withdrawal from the demanding daily round. The pilgrims are reminded here of the need for balance in our lives, for making and taking opportunities for prayer and meditation to enable us to cope with our business and responsibilities. For the next stage of the Pilgrimage people are invited to walk in silence.

The next stop, on the top of Dun-I, as mentioned at the beginning of Chapter 2, is a mountain-top experience with splendid views in all directions when visibility is clear. High winds and driving rain sometimes make speaking and hearing difficult, but here the theme is new perspectives and the possibility of new purpose and meaning, strengthened commitment to follow in the way of the risen Christ, full of potential surprises and often entailing risk-taking in engagement with the struggles and pains of the world.

The last stop is St Oran's Chapel, the oldest building on Iona, supposed to have been built at the request of Queen Margaret in the twelfth century. It may seem strange to end the Pilgrimage in a graveyard but for Christians death is not the end, and here people are encouraged to think about resurrection and new life, moving on to the next stage of their journey beyond Iona with a sense of vision and hope, open to one another and to the new possibilities to which God is calling us.

The Pilgrimage is at the heart of the Iona experience not only because of its timing in the middle of the week – often indeed at a critical point in the programme when the some of the novelty has worn off and people are starting to ask difficult questions! The Pilgrimage is also an integrated and integrating embodiment of the Community's understanding of and approach to spirituality – described before as 'an energising kind of connectedness'. It has been spoken of by Peter Millar as 'for many people a tremendous powerful spiritual experience in which God often speaks to them in new ways'. It affords opportunities, within a framework of worship and sharing, for reflecting and exploring, for discussing new ideas and old, for forging and deepening relationships, for discerning and engaging with the struggles of the world and the purposes and promises of God, for looking to the future as the journey goes on.

O helper of workers,
ruler of all the good,
guard on the ramparts
and defender of the faithful,
who lift up the lowly
and crush the proud,
ruler of the faithful,
enemy of the impenitent,
judge of all judges,
who punish those who err,
pure life of the living,
light and Father of lights
shining with great light,
denying to none of the hopeful
your strength and help,
I beg that me, a little man
trembling and most wretched,
rowing through the infinite storm
of this age,
Christ may draw after Him to the lofty
most beautiful haven of life
. . . an unending
holy hymn forever.

From the envy of enemies you lead me
into the joy of paradise.
through you, Christ Jesus,
who live and reign . . .

(From Thomas Owen Clancy and Gilbert Márkus, *Iona – The Earliest Poetry of a Celtic Monastery*, (attributed to St Columba))

'A place of hope,'
They say:
and in their thousands
they journey, year by year,
to this tiny island
on the margins of Europe.
Sunswept and windswept,
yet always deeply
a place of transformation.
A sacred spot on earth:
a pilgrim's place
of light and shadow
energy and challenge.

We need you, Iona,
with your alternative vision,
with your ever-present questions
your often uncomfortable silence.

For you are a place of prayer,
of Christ's abiding:
weaving a rainbow of meaning
through the endless busyness of our days,
holding together the frayed threads
of our fleeting devotion
opening a path for healing
and for peace.

Not momentary healing
nor easy faith,
but struggle, commitment,
and an ongoing conversion
are your gifts for
our broken yet beautiful lives.
(Peter Millar, *An Iona Prayer Book*)

6

The Community's Mainland Work

Each week on Iona the broader context and the relation of what happens at the islands centres to the wider work of the Iona Community are emphasised – both in the regular programme sessions for guests and the talks about the Community given to day-visitors after the Sunday morning Communion, and in the opportunities given on Sunday morning and at the Thursday evening commitment service to contribute for this purpose through the offerings. Many people, however, especially those who understandably identify the Iona Community with Iona, are surprised to discover that there is more to the Community's work than what goes on on Iona itself and that the Community's headquarters are in Glasgow. The administrative base, after periods in different locations, as mentioned in an earlier chapter, is now situated in Govan, on the top floor of the Pearce Institute, a community centre and monument to Victorian philanthropy (as the gift of a shipping magnate's widow), which is run as an independent trust but was formerly directly associated with Govan Old parish church from which George MacLeod resigned to found the Community. Although this is the centre of the organisation, and where the mainland outreach project workers have their official home, there is nonetheless no sense in which it is regarded as any more significant than the islands centres or indeed than the publishing department, which owing to lack of space moved a few years ago to occupy several rooms in a disused school nearby which had been converted to provide work-space for a range of small businesses. And in any case for many years the Community has affirmed that the most important part of its mainland work is what Members do, and indeed Associate Members too, in their own local situations, through their work and other activities, to pursue the concerns of the Community and live out their commitment where they are. The connections among all these strands of the Community's life, and the extent to which they are part of a single entity, coherent and yet dynamic, clearly reflect once again the undergirding integrated approach to spirituality.

These links between Glasgow and Iona and between Glasgow and the Members in dispersion (as indeed the links between the Members and Iona) are of critical significance, and it is necessary to ensure that the communication of information is effective not only to keep the organisation running as smoothly as possible but also as an expression of mutual respect, common ownership and accountability. This applies equally among both staff and Members: the sense of belonging together and 'going somewhere' with a common purpose does not just 'happen'; attention needs to be given to developing processes that are as open and inclusive as possible.

The issue of worship in the mainland office provides an interesting and illuminating insight into how the Community's spirituality is expressed in practice. By way of background it is perhaps instructive to remember that certain church organisations do insist that their employees must have both a Christian commitment and a live church connection, although the Church of Scotland's Board of Social Responsibility has recently been challenged, on equal opportunities grounds, about operating such a policy in its social work establishments. And the

Community itself requires its islands resident staff, all of whom have to play a regular part in planning and leading worship, to share the Community's Christian commitment. But nothing on these lines is prescribed in relation to mainland staff: as in the case of volunteers on Iona they are simply expected to be in sympathy with the concerns and purposes of the Community to the extent of being content to work for it.

Since the move from Community House in Clyde Street, where the circumstances were very different and daily worship in the chapel was a public occasion, the possibility of worship in the mainland office has been raised, considered and attempted from time to time, because of certain staff members' wish that it should happen and also not least because of the Community's commitment to the centrality of worship in relation to other aspects of life and work. Apart from problems concerning the practical arrangements, on account of the working patterns of outreach staff and thus the recurrent absence of some of those committed to holding worship, one of the issues that has figured prominently in the discussion has been the potential divisiveness of an activity from which some of the staff inevitably will choose to exclude themselves. The building of community is a complex business (the annual debate about the nature and venue of the staff Christmas outing is shot through with similar difficulties!); and the responses in the Community's office (and the Iona morning liturgy) 'Love and faith come together/Justice and peace join hands' – take on fresh nuances! It is a matter of energy, ethos and purpose, of expressing belief through practice, of how to balance conviction and a compassionate generosity of spirit. So far we seem to be managing: for the meantime, at least at the point of writing, the mainland worship continues without any obvious adverse effects on staff dynamics or morale.

'The mainland work of the Community is first and foremost what its individual Members do in their own situations.' So said the Community's booklet *What is the Iona Community?*

first published in the 1980s and issued again, in a revised edition, in 1996. As has been indicated earlier, this has been the Community's thinking and intention since the outset; but inevitably, where there are staff with specific responsibilities in fields which are fundamental to the Community's purpose and concerns, the significance of the role of Members can be reduced, at least in some people's eyes. However, the fact that the Community has for many years had a member of staff (sometimes indeed more than one) working with young people and youth groups, on both Iona and the mainland, does not mean that that person somehow represents the sum total of the Community's interest or expertise in the field of youth work: many Members have previous experience and retain close interest and involvement; for others this may be their occupation, whether in church or secular employment, or a leisure-time commitment.

Similarly, for over a decade the Community employed a full-time worker whose remit originally related to development education but was subsequently changed to focus more generally on justice and peace. The worker concerned, Helen Steven, is herself a Community Member, a former school-teacher who became thoroughly conscientised as a political activist and peace campaigner after working with the Quakers in Vietnam. There has been a tendency at times for her to be regarded as the instigator of all the Community's justice and peace activities, with the resulting danger of other Members somehow being let off the hook; and this has only diminished through the passage of time and with further adjustment of the working arrangements so as to involve joint support, with the Quakers, of the centre – Peace House, near Dunblane – where she was based until recently.

And again, in relation to worship, which will be explored more fully in the next chapter, the pioneering work and well-deserved, outstanding reputation of the Wild Goose Resource Group, in developing new, more participative approaches to the creation and leading of worship and in producing a whole range of liturgical material, songs, prayers, sketches, using more familiar and accessible language than is the currency of traditional hymns and services, can lead to the experience and gifts of others being neglected and forgotten. In fact the principles that underlie the work of the Wild Goose Resource Group, and the approach to liturgy that they are developing, have been part of the Community's life, indeed of it spirituality, since the outset. And there are many Members, not only ordained ministers, who are recognised within the wider Church as having particular skills in the field of liturgy: Douglas Galbraith is Secretary of the Church of Scotland's Panel on Worship and a former university lecturer in this area; Donald McIlhagga has been editing a new hymn anthology for the millennium and has been prominent in liturgy committees of the United Reformed Church; among others Anna Briggs, Ruth Burgess, Tom Colvin, Ian Cowie, Leith Fisher, Ian Fraser, Kathy Galloway, Kate McIlhagga, Mary Pearson and Jan Sutch Pickard have had their hymns and prayers included in collections (published by bodies other than the Community!), and almost one-third of the songs contained in the new book *Common Ground* published in 1997 by the Scottish churches are by Members and Associates of the Community.

So it is an essential part of the belonging together in community and of our shared understanding of our spirituality, our energising relationship with God and one another, that Members pursue the concerns of the Community and put the Rule into practice in whatever way is most appropriate in their own situation. And of course there is a wide and wonderful diversity in these situations! With two hundred Members in Britain, together with a dozen overseas, even the geographical range is considerable, although, as might be expected in view of the Community's history, the greatest concentration is in the central belt of Scotland. Similarly there is a wide variety of personal circumstances, occupational backgrounds, working settings, and other commitments. Members' ages range from several now in their eighties to some in their twenties; and it is not necessarily the youngest who are most active!

For the last twenty years or so the Community has had certain specifically identified areas of concern on which to focus its work and witness. Previously there had been both ad hoc initiatives and continuing issues, for which Members would form groups. At the time when I became a full Member of the Community in 1980 there were three major working groups – work and the new economic order; justice and peace; community and celebration – and there was also a separate youth planning group to develop the Community's policy for its work among young people both on Iona and the mainland. As I understand it, these three groups, with their rather grandiose titles, emerged from discussion among Members at plenary meetings: the topics reflected perceptions of what were major issues for church and society (and therefore for the Community corporately and for Members in their local situations) and particular Members' interests at the time. The intention was that each Member would belong to one of the groups although it was recognised that other commitments and geography would prevent a number of Members from attending meetings with any regularity. The function of the groups was both to provide an opportunity for sharing common concerns and developing thinking, and to influence the life, priorities and policy of the Community. Taken together, in the context once more of these recurring themes of engagement, connectedness and spirituality, the fields covered by the groups might have been seen to embrace most of the Community's work and concerns. In practice, like so much else they worked with a certain unevenness – good at times, good in parts!

I was a member of the Justice and Peace Planning Group and very clearly recall highly stimulating, rather badly attended discussions on the question whether, following up Members' commitment under the Community's Rule to action for justice and peace, opposition to nuclear weapons should be made a confessional issue, using the Barmen Declaration of the German churches during the Second World War as a model. My recollection of the outcome of our deliberations is much less clear – except that nothing came of the idea, partly because the Scottish churches at the time were themselves moving towards a firmer official line, culminating in an emotionally charged reconciliation at the 1988 General Assembly of the Church of Scotland between George MacLeod, who had been campaigning unsuccessfully on this for years, and one of his most intractable opponents, who declared himself converted, and the Kirk itself went on to approve a resolution to the effect that there was no moral or theological justification for such weapons. Significantly it was when the Kirk addressed the spiritual and theological dimension of this debate, to which George MacLeod and other Community Members had been directing attention for years, that the formal view shifted.

In the late 1980s, after an extended period of discussion, as already mentioned in Chapter 1, the Community agreed on a 'strategic plan', an appraisal of structures and directions, and an identification of working priorities for the ensuing period. One of the outcomes was the replacement of the three previous working groups, indeed of the approach on which they were based, with a different kind of arrangement involving six 'areas of concern', agreed by the Community as focal issues for work and witness through the nineties. An additional one was created shortly afterwards, to reflect the Community's interest in the discussions surrounding the possibility of a Scottish Parliament and other constitutional issues; and a review of the strategic plan was completed in 1996, after a careful and inclusive consultation process, added three further areas. The ten areas are: ecumenical issues, with the title 'Called to be one' (originally 'sharing communion by the year 2000'); justice, peace and the integrity of creation; racism matters; rediscovery of spirituality; the cause of the poor and the exploited; youth concern (formerly 'youth planning group' in direct succession to the original group); democracy; work and unemployment issues; sexuality; and inter-religious relations.

There is clearly a degree of overlap among some of these areas, for example, a number relate to what might be regarded as justice issues, and relevant questions have to be asked about reducing the areas of concern, on the basis that the Community can only reasonably manage so much, and the dropping of an area signifies current priorities rather than the abandonment of concern. There is also a need to develop some kind of coherent strategy within which the different areas can dovetail. The spread of the areas is an obvious reflection of the scope of the Community's concerns and the nature of its spirituality, both the historical roots of the Community and contemporary imperatives. We engage in these areas neither instead of nor in opposition to other groups, Christian or secular, and increasingly we recognise the practical value and prophetic significance of networking, alliance-building and joint action with other groups, church-related or not, that share the Community's values and objectives.

It would appear that the original idea was that each area of concern would have a co-ordinator, with overall responsibility, and that within each area there might be several groups, based either on geography or around sub-topics under the general heading. As with so much else within the life of the Community, things have developed rather differently from expected – and the flexibility, openness to changing opportunities and possibilities, and sense of provisionality this reveals are not without relevance to the Community's approach to spirituality. Most of the areas do have a working group of Members who have a particular commitment or interest in that field, but there is no uniform pattern to the size or working arrangements of the various groups: their approaches depend partly on what Members belong to them, partly on the nature and demands of the particular area. In some cases there is an active nucleus that meets regularly and a wider group of 'corresponding members'; but some groups, especially the newer ones, are essentially networks who may meet only on special occasions, often in conjunction with a Members' plenary meeting, for example during Community Week on Iona in the summer.

The intention, already achieved in some measure, is that the groups should inform and influence the work and life of the Community in a variety of ways – through, for example, raising awareness within the Community relating to issues within the area of concern by discussion at plenary meetings or *Coracle* articles; through making recommendations to the Community's Council or committees for policy initiatives; through providing advice on matters where the Community may seek to influence the churches or the Government; through input to the Iona programme; through supporting and developing Members' personal involvement in the area; and through networking with other groups and organisations with similar concerns.

This last point is of special significance. The primary purpose of the working groups is internal to the life of the Community – to gather together people who are activists or have an interest in a specific area with a view to enhancing the Community's awareness or commitment. They are not intended to be separate campaigning groups, because there are already other organisations involved in all these fields, and the Community is formally affiliated to many of these, such as Church Action on Poverty, World Development Movement, Campaign for Nuclear Disarmament, Action for Southern Africa, Scottish Civic Assembly, Real World Coalition. There is no virtue in the Community duplicating what such bodies are doing. Within the new political culture of 'civil society' that is emerging within Britain, and that flourished especially in Scotland during the 'Thatcher' years, such alliances and coalitions, which may focus only on a single issue and have a limited life-span, have a central function.

Given the Community's engaged and inclusive

understanding of spirituality there will always be a temptation, at both corporate and personal levels, to be active on too many fronts at once, to take on more than resources of time, energy, and money can responsibly cope with. Given the commitment to the integration and connectedness that are the heart of the spirituality, the challenge is to hold it all together in ways that have direction and coherence and to ensure effective communication and co-ordination among the different parts. Within the life of the Community there will thus always be a multi-faceted character about the work and commitments, and there will always be a debate about priorities, both about the possibility of new projects and new areas of concern, reflecting particular interests and gifts and responding to particular needs, and about the need not to spread resources too thinly, to dissipate energy and efforts, but rather to maximise effectiveness by concentrating deliberately on a well-defined limited number of areas. Such discussions are an intrinsic part of the Community's life, both as movement and as organisation, and flow naturally from the incarnational theology and the spirituality of engagement.

Some reference was made in the previous chapter to the changing pattern of the Community's corporate mainland work over the years. George MacLeod expressed the Community's fundamental missionary commitment memorably in terms of 'rebuilding the common life'. It is perhaps a sign of our times, with the widespread interest in personal growth and the significance of the senses and the emotions, that we have generally described our purpose as seeking and exploring 'new ways to touch the hearts of all'. The emphasis may appear different, but there is no essential inconsistency, for the thrust is towards the discovery and embodiment of a spirituality that gives energy and inspiration, rooted in an engagement and encounter with God in the midst of the world. The vision is the universal community of harmony, justice, love and peace, the fullness of life promised to all and conclusively revealed through Jesus Christ; the calling is to share in God's transforming and healing work through which the vision is being realised as the kingdom breaks through into our world.

In our own modest way, often hesitant and faltering, sometimes taking risks with deep breaths, frequently not getting it right, ready to laugh at ourselves, the Community has not been afraid to develop new initiatives in its mainland work and to find resources, whether from within its own funds when this is possible or by approaching grant-making bodies, to finance these. In the years following the Second World War, the Community had a strong and obvious commitment to the exploration of new approaches to parish ministry, especially in the so-called 'church extension charges' which were introduced by the Church of Scotland's new housing schemes, and to other innovative forms of ministry. The first industrial chaplains in Scotland were Community Members; and Members were the first wardens of two new church centres, Scottish Churches House, Dunblane and Carberry Tower, near Edinburgh, where there was pioneering work in relating the Gospel to contemporary issues – those concerned, Ian Fraser and Colin Day respectively, are still Members of the Community, both now in their eighties. Alongside projects like these, the theology and spirituality embodied in the work on Iona was expressed through the range of imaginative and trail-blazing projects based at Community House, strong traces of which are still deeply embedded in the life of the Community, both in the oral tradition and through the people who were involved, many of whom are still Members or otherwise supportively associated with the Community.

After the closure of Community House, during Ron Ferguson's term as Leader, several new projects were developed. Following a proposal to the Church of Scotland's General Assembly that was unsuccessful only by a narrow majority, Walter Fyfe, then a Community Member and formerly a member of the Gorbals Group, with which the

Community had had close links, was appointed to undertake work in relation to the pressing issue of unemployment. To fund this work, which involved helping local communities to set up food co-operatives and credit unions as well as promoting awareness and debate about unemployment issues both within the Community and beyond, the Community sold most of its collection of valuable paintings, including several of Iona by the famous 'Scottish colourists'.

Other initiatives included the setting up of a justice and peace resource centre, along with Christian Aid and the Balmore Trust, in the city centre of Glasgow to sell Third World crafts and raise awareness of development issues. At this time too the Community supported and encouraged 'Columban Houses', described by Ron Ferguson in *Chasing the Wild Goose* as 'a low key experiment . . . designed to explore new models of Christian community in urban situations . . . with the declared aim of incarnating the concerns of the Iona Community'. There was no single blueprint for a Columban House, a few of which were established also beyond Scotland: there were different living arrangements, whether, for example, a community of people in a single house, or neighbours coming together for particular purposes, but the common focus was sharing, hospitality and the links with the Community and its concerns.

The youth work at this time was co-ordinated by John Bell and Graham Maule under a work-sharing arrangement. They developed a scheme for youth volunteers, living (usually in a Columban House) and working in areas of urban deprivation, linking in with the work of the centres on Iona. Out of this also emerged the Wild Goose Worship Group, still active today and now sixteen-strong. It contributes in association with the Wild Goose Resource Group, to the shaping of new ways to worship through workshops, special services and conferences, and events like 'Last Night Out' which takes place in a city-centre church in Glasgow on the last Sunday of each month, except over the summer, and draws people of all ages to worship and take part in a series of workshops on contemporary issues of faith and life.

The Community also at this time took forward its commitment to exploring new methods of training for lay ministry through the development of a radical and imaginative scheme called 'Peregrini' after the ancient Celtic monks, wandering on mission and pilgrimage in a bygone era. Two of the former youth volunteers undertook a year's programme of experiential learning in challenging situations on the mainland followed by a spell on Iona before proceeding to other forms of ministry.

But with changing circumstances and personnel, and questions about the availability of resources and arrangements for funding, the Community's priorities shifted, and it is interesting to reflect on the fact that none of these projects survives from only fifteen years or so ago, with the exception of the Columban Houses, of which, however, only a few remain. This is not because they 'failed' – much was achieved and experienced that was very worthwhile. It has to do rather with a sense of the provisionality and movement that is at the heart of the Community's understanding of spirituality, the recognition that often it is time to let go and journey on.

More recently two outreach workers were employed on a part-time, short-term basis with remits that related to pastoral and educational work in the local area. In this can be perceived something of a dilemma that faces the Community with its commitment to a spirituality of engagement: what is the area, who the people we are to engage with? At present all the mainland staff with outreach responsibilities have no particular local focus; all work nationally, some internationally. As the Community considers the possibility of a new mainland base, with additional space to accommodate staff together in a way that is more convenient, more conducive to community-building, and more hospitable to visitors, issues of location have to be weighed up. For example; the best place for a sales outlet would almost certainly not be the kind of area with which the Community, with its commitment to solidarity with those who are disadvantaged, would most readily identify. Also the possibility of further local outreach projects must be allowed for, although some would argue that, whatever the historical precedents, it is for the Members themselves to undertake the *local* work, and the function of the mainland staff is to operate on a wider, broader canvas.

Thus the role of the Community's youth worker, as the job title clearly indicates, is youth-*development* work. Part of this work is related to the Community's activities on Iona, in terms of preparation and follow-up with young people, whether in groups or as individuals, visiting the islands centres, and the running of specific events on Iona, most notably the annual Youth Festival, or sometimes at Camas, which is geared for young people. But another important part of the work, which Ruth Clements, the present post-holder, has developed very effectively, is the promotion of the Community's concerns through networking and involvement in young people's events with other bodies and workers in this field – some within the churches, some in church-related organisations, others with no direct church connections. Much of the work, either explicitly or by implication, involves the exploration of an appropriate spirituality for young people in today's world. And it is significant that, in a recent document about the strategy of the Community's mainland youth work, Ruth Clements has identified its distinctive characteristics in a way that clearly, though more or less unconsciously, relates to a spirituality of engagement and connectedness. There is an intrinsic flexibility, a readiness to work both at grass roots and at national level, an ecumenical impartiality, and a genuine attempt to relate faith to the issues of life. The work is rooted in the experience, history and ethos of Iona, Camas and the Community generally and, flowing naturally from that, provides opportunities for the Church to meet the secular world and for the exploration of the Community's concerns. Finally the Community's youth work offers alternative models and methodologies of being and working, a place where diverse views can be examined in a context of balance and accountability, issues of values and identity are struggled with, and the possibility of change recognised.

As with so much else within the life of the Community, with its youth work there is a sense of living on the edge, of the kind of risk and open-endedness that is an intrinsic part of the spiritual perspective. It is an inescapable fact that the former youth camps on Iona attracted many more young people than go to Iona now, and the views of many older Members have more to do with personal recollections of the past than with the present realities of the postmodern world and contemporary youth culture. There are plenty of challenges ahead here and those involved in the youth concern working group are continuing to feed suggestions into the Community about policy, priorities and possibilities so as to enable the engagement with young people to continue.

Similarly, the Community's perspective on spirituality is a strong theme of the Wild Goose Resource Group, already mentioned several times, whose approach will be considered more fully in the next chapter which deals directly with worship. One of the Resource Group, John Bell, has an international reputation as a modern hymn-writer and as a speaker about liturgy and spirituality. Along with that of his colleague and co-author Graham Maule his work has appeared in almost every recent collection of hymns published in the English-speaking world. Consistently with what has already been said about the Community's understanding of spirituality, John Bell emphasises the importance of the communal dimension: spirituality is not 'a matter of private preference' but of 'public accountability', as practised, almost counter-culturally, according to the Community's Rule. He describes spirituality as 'the expression of our personal relationship with

God' and distinguishes its characteristics, echoing themes already explored above, as incarnational ('the antidote to contemporary escapist religion'), holistic (recognising the integrity and connectedness of all things), catholic (inclusive and thus exposed to the influence of the world Church), and radical (rooted in the Bible, 'allowing the injunctions of God's word to inform and judge our activity in the contemporary world').

The Community's understanding of spirituality is expressed also through the other parts of its mainland work, not least perhaps through the activities of the administrative and financial staff without whose considerable efforts both organisation and movement would collapse: they make many of the connections and sustain the connectedness which enables the engagement to happen; here above all there is a sense of the down-to-earth, sometimes even of 'God in the midst'. Rather more obviously the Community's spirituality is reflected in the pages of *Coracle*, the Community's bi-monthly magazine, still retaining the original name, but for the last ten years or so in a format that contains both news of people and events and a range of articles and poems relating to the Community's purpose, concerns and activities. And the Community's publishing department, Wild Goose Publications, has an expanding output of books, pamphlets, recordings and worship resources which, in reflecting the liturgical, theological and social interests of the Community, cast light also on its spirituality.

An instructive insight both into 'how others see us' and the essence of the Community's approach to spirituality was provided in March 1997, when the Community published *A Very British Monster*, a rather controversial pamphlet, written by Stanley Hope, convener of the racism area of concern working group, about the shortcomings of Britain's immigration policies and the need for the reform of nationality law. One of the local London radio stations asked what on earth the Community was doing venturing into this sort of field when it was so noted for its work in relation to liturgy and spirituality! It remains broadly true that in England and America the Community tends to be associated with worship and Celtic spirituality, whereas, mitigated slightly by the growing reputation of the Wild Goose Resource Group (less and less 'prophets without honour in their own land'), in Scotland the Community (because of the lasting impact made by George MacLeod) is still regarded as having more to do with a very left-wing brand of politics than with religion! The truth of course is that a spirituality of engagement draws all these different strands together.

Jim Wallis, of the Sojourners Community in Washington DC, in whose commitment to the integration of social justice and spirituality there are clear affinities with the Iona Community, has said, 'The marks of grace are gentleness, hope and faith. The most dependable sign of its presence is joy.' The life and spirituality of the Community is perhaps to be described as generous rather than gentle, but there is certainly much laughter to accompany the hope and the faith, much joy in belonging together, and a deeper quality in the sharing and mutuality that has to do with both perception and persistence. Erik Cramb sums it up in his appreciation of

> the power of stories and observation or 'feel' that, though we work at it in the Community, we are undoubtedly encouraged by the sense of 'the thin place' [a reference to George MacLeod's already quoted description of the feeling on Iona of the 'tissue-thin' distinction between heaven and earth, the spiritual and the material] to see things like, for example, the incredible persistence of a dandelion pushing itself through tarmac – and we learn to make stories about life pushing through tarmac – and we learn to make stories about life pushing through death, the dead tarmac of secularisation and materialism. And perhaps we are more inclined to talk about dandelions

than about the more romantic daisy. I remember one of the first things that struck me about Alice Scrimgeour [a remarkable Church of Scotland deaconness, now retired, very influential within the life of the Community, but never a Member, owing to women being excluded from membership until 1969] not setting out to 'improve' the youngsters who came to her camps, just 'enjoying' them – the ability to love a dandelion as much as a daisy, and when you say that logic says, 'Why not?'

Holy God, into your hands we commit this day; may we move freely where it takes us, where your spirit leads.
Holy God, into your hands we commend this place; may we rejoice in its liveliness and light, ponder its darkness and shadows.
Holy God, into your hands we commend those around us, friends and strangers here by our side, colleagues and loved ones farther away.
Holy God, into your hands we commend ourselves, a little unsure but eager, a little restless but still.
We, here on Iona, join with members and associates round the world in praying and being concerned about young people in our communities.
God, blow your spirit into those who work with young people.
Help them keep their silence when a teenager needs to find his or her own words.
Help them choose their words carefully when a young person asks for help or advice.
Keep them strong when they lack support in facing constant struggles and don't know what the answer is.
Let them enjoy the small moments.
God, be with young people travelling to Iona in the coming year. Rain your words upon them; water them as the seeds of hope we all are, to grow up into the sunlight

and live in the joy of knowing that they, like us here, are unique and special. Open their minds to those they will meet here on Iona and to the new ideas and songs they will hear. Let them sing their soul and cry their tears and know that you are.

God, travel with each young visitor and volunteer like the pebbles in their pockets, small and round, shiny and beautiful, something to hold on to in the tight fist of their hand.

Likewise strengthen all who as youth associates, members and staff through the Iona Community articulate spirituality and belief in the unbelievable to young people struggling to exist in a contradictory and inhospitable world.

We pray for all young people who struggle in our cities, to find their place, hold their own, even to feel just OK. May they catch a glimpse of something better – of a topsy-turvy kingdom where the last come first. May they have hope.

(Ruth Clements, March 1998, Iona)

7

The Centrality of Worship

It is interesting that, whereas twenty years ago the Iona Community was best known, at any rate in Scotland, for its political campaigning and in many people's eyes would have been seen on most issues as taking a rather extreme stance that had little or nothing to do with religion and worship, now within contemporary church circles almost anywhere in the world, where there is any awareness at all of the Iona Community, it is likely to be in connection with or in the context of worship. This is in part testimony to the impact made by the work of the Wild Goose Resource Group over the last decade or so, in their contribution to the development and renewal of worship within the life of the churches – through worship events, workshops and conferences, usually ecumenical, around Britain, and particularly the annual Schools of Music and Worship held on Iona and now also in the north of England; through new hymns and other liturgical resources, published by the Iona Community and included also in many other collections; through broadcasting, most notably perhaps the last 9.30 a.m. morning service on Radio 4 in March 1998, which evoked a huge, highly appreciative response. Overseas especially, the reputation of John Bell as lecturer and facilitator, in both denominational and ecumenical liturgical circles, consistently gives rise to more invitations – particularly from America and Australia – than can be accepted. And more recently the launch, at introductory events around Scotland, of the new and extremely popular ecumenical song book *Common Ground*, in which John (as convener of the Editorial Committee, and former convener of the Church of Scotland's Panel on Worship) was prominently involved, has broadened the Resource Group's contacts with Scottish congregations.

But the association of the Iona Community with worship is probably due above all to people's experience of worship on Iona itself. Kathy Galloway has said that 'the worship of the Iona Community is the backbone of its embodied and integrated spirituality'. This could be put another way: the Community's spirituality is not only embodied and expressed in its worship; it is also embedded in it. From the very outset worship has lain at the heart of the Community's life and concerns. Whenever Members of the Community gather, whether in Family Groups or at plenary meetings, they worship together. The daily life on Iona begins and ends with worship; but the significance of worship within the rhythm of the life of the Community, and particularly of life on Iona, runs much deeper than that.

Best-seller among the Community's publications is the book entitled *The Iona Community Worship Book*. The title is misleading: it is in fact a collection of the liturgies used in the cycle of services each week on Iona, including also a range of alternative possibilities for certain services and resources for specific services. It is immensely popular both because many people want a memento of a memorable, and often challenging, worship experience and because of the considerable demand for material and resources that can be used and adapted for other occasions and circumstances. The book, currently into its third impression, was published in 1990, itself a revised edition of an earlier version; and the need is now recognised to bring it up to date once more in a way that reflects the variety and creativity of the current worship and certain further developments that have taken place. As the introduction to the book explains, from the start the Community's integrated spirituality permeated the common life so that work and worship were and still are seen as all of a piece. God's purpose is the reconciliation and unity of all created things to the point where, as one of George MacLeod's marvellous soaring prayers says, 'The whole earth shall cry glory'. As a Community, although inevitably we do not live it out as effectively as we should, 'we are committed to the belief that worship is all that we are . . . and everything we do, both inside and outside the church, so that our whole lives are an act of worship, an offering to God'. So in the liturgy used regularly in morning worship on Iona, we say 'we shall not offer to God offerings that cost us nothing', and the service ends without a benediction since people disperse to carry out their daily tasks, including the chores undertaken by the guests at our centres, and the blessing does not come until the close of the evening service twelve hours or so later.

In a very challenging paper contributing to the continuing discussion about the future of the Community's islands centres, John Harvey gives an extended personal insight, in the context of his experience both as former Leader of the Community and as Abbey Warden in the early 1970s, into how the place of worship on Iona may have changed as a result of the external pressures:

> The great gift that I feel I have received from the Iona Community – from God – is the expression, in the Community's life, of the central Christian insight into the integrity of worship. We have long put this into words by using the phrase about 'work and worship'. But it's worth more than that. For me the excitement of Iona, when I first came here, was discovering that not only was 'worship' not simply what religious people did in church,

but that worship was everything that Christian disciples did and offered to God, and that this could be expressed in a style of living open and accessible to anyone, anywhere.

On Iona, in the building days, this insight was of course expressed in the context appropriate to that stage in the life of the Community. Thus, each day, men came to the morning service in their working clothes – and consciously saw their work on the walls as their daily worship. Minister-members each day both shared in the work on the walls and took part in what was called 'ministers' craftmanship – lectures, discussions, sermon preparation, etc. All this was 'worth-ship': services were part of that, and needed to be prepared and led well – but they were only *part* of worship, never the whole thing.

In expressing the integrity of worship in this way, at that time, the Community was making some significant statements. It was saying something significant, for instance, about what *church* worship should be about: about God, certainly, but about God Incarnate, and about God's world, this world. But it was also saying something it, and the significant about daily life – that all life is sacred, and that the living of it, and the work done in it, was as much an offering to God as anything done in church.

Also, it's important that we remember that, at that time, the real focus of the Community's concerns was not Iona, but mainland Britain and the wider world. Ralph Morton [Deputy Leader to George MacLeod] said once – he may have said it many times! – that any real experimenting, in liturgy or in anything else, could never really happen on Iona: it had to happen on the mainland, in the context of daily life of the world 'out there'. What the Community tried to do on Iona, in liturgy or in anything else, was truly 'for export only'!

John Harvey goes on to set the Community's approach to worship in the context of its developing work on Iona following the completion of the rebuilding of the Abbey and in particular of the 'conscious decision to set up a "proper" resident group', i.e., one established as a conscious act of will on the part of the whole Community.

> The thinking behind this new phase in the life of the Community was this. The Community's central thrust, of the integrity of worship as I have described it, would be maintained. In place of the 'worship' of the daily work on the walls would be the 'worship' of hospitality: the craftspeople here on Iona would no longer be rebuilding walls but rebuilding people – and this would be our offering to God in this place. And this, as far as I am aware, is the underpinning rationale behind the maintenance of a resident group on Iona.

John then refers to the changes that have taken place over the subsequent years – the vast increase in the number of people coming to Iona; the growing difficulty experienced by the Community in recruiting staff (of whom many more are now needed as the scale of the operation has grown) with the same vision as when the resident group model was begun; the fact that,

> partly due to the success of the Wild Goose Resource Group, the Iona Community is best known now for its liturgies, which are loosely referred to as 'worship' – to such an extent, for instance, that one hears of 'Iona worship' happening up and down the country, as if it was some sort of self-standing happening quite unconnected to daily life! The Abbey services are now increasingly seen either (by our guests and by holiday-makers) as similar self-standing events (and judged as such) or

(increasingly by staff and even by Members) as no longer expressing the 'worth-ship' of their daily life and work. Thus the integrity of worship is actually being threatened by our presence and practice on Iona!

In Camas a few years ago, the Chapel of the Nets was dismantled, rather to many people's dismay! This was done partly in a conscious attempt to reclaim the integrity of worship. So each week each group was invited to construct its own chapel – some even decided not to have one at all, and to hold their services either in the dining-room or in the open air. This was much harder work than simply continuing to use the Chapel of the Nets, with all its hallowed (but by then largely forgotten) associations. But it could be argued that doing it the new way was more in keeping with the Community's initial insights – especially as Camas is really the only one of the three islands centres where the Community still was able to maintain control over who came to it. In other words, at Camas the Community could still call the shots, both in terms of who came and in terms of what happened while they were there.

This puts very well the essence of the challenge that faces the Community in maintaining its witness and seeking to shape its future life and priorities. Worship remains both in theory and reality the mainspring of our life together as a Community, and of all our activities, and both the beginning and end of our commitment to world peace, social justice and the rediscovery of an integrated spirituality. On Iona, as the scale of activities and numbers of people have grown, there is inevitably an increased sense of worship as a public inclusive event, even a performance or spectacle, rather than an experience. With this growth it is often hard to hold on to the perspective that worship is our whole rounded daily experience of which the events are only a part, and thus, at least in relation to worship, there is undoubtedly a risk that something of the interconnectedness that is fundamental to this spirituality may be diluted or even lost.

It is true, as John Harvey says, that at Camas, because of its distinctive setting and more intimate character, things are still possible that cannot any longer be contemplated and achieved on Iona. At Camas in recent years, as a result of a combination of the closeness to nature, the simple and fairly spartan facilities, and the perspective of the leaders of the staff group, there has been a particular emphasis on exploring, within a generally holistic approach, the ecological dimensions of spirituality. Few of the groups coming to Camas these days are either familiar or comfortable with traditional, or perhaps any, patterns of Christian worship. At the start of the week the general ethos, programme and facilities are explained to them and they are invited to 'create' the Chapel of the Nets, where most of the morning and evening reflections take place. These take the form of meditations and explorations, led creatively by members of the Camas staff, using Christian and other resources, and relating closely to other aspects of the week's experience.

Inevitably daily worship on Iona is a little more conventional than at Camas, in terms of both location and content. But it encompasses a huge diversity of themes and experiences, memorable for so many people in so many different ways – whether for the challenge a particular service contains, for the exposure to new songs, new insights, or a generally new approach to worship, or for a particular experience on a specific occasion. There may be nothing quite like the sun streaming in through the great east window of the Abbey church during a morning service, or the sound and feel of the wind howling outside on a Sunday evening quiet time, or the Holy Week services, with the church crowded to overflowing – the Saturday night Easter vigil as the light breaks through the darkness, or the joy of the Easter morning Communion; or a winter's night in the Michael Chapel, cosy and candle-lit, where the staff worship in winter when the big Abbey church is closed: so many individuals have their own vivid, very personal recollections.

The daily worship on Iona is based on the life of the continuing staff group along with the guests at the Community's centres. The work and activities of this community of staff and guests which forms and reforms each week is both framed by and rooted in worship. Through this worship our accountability, for all that we say and do and are, is expressed and our common story is told and reflected upon – both the immediate story of the week's experience and, however unfashionable it may be in these 'postmodern' times, the salvation-history that directs our common task and shapes our common life.

The daily worship on Iona follows a regular pattern but within that there is great variety. The morning services are based on a set responsive liturgy of songs, prayers and readings, which has elements in common with the Community's 'office' that is normally used when Members gather; there are also certain parts – the Bible readings, one of the songs, parts of the prayers – which change each day; and the prayers of intercession include prayers by name for Members of the Community based on a monthly cycle used by them in their own daily prayer wherever they are.

The evening worship also follows a pattern, this time weekly, which reflects both the rhythm of the week in the centres and in turn different aspects of the concerns of the Community – Saturday welcome; Sunday quiet time, with opportunity for *ex tempore* prayer by the congregation; Monday prayers for peace and justice; Tuesday prayers for personal and political healing; Wednesday a service prepared by guests in one of the centres, often with a focus on the integrity of creation; Thursday an opportunity to make an act of commitment, recognising the significance of personal accountability; Friday an informal celebration of Holy Communion around long tables stretching in front of the choir stalls. These services, with the exception of the Wednesday evening guest service, are prepared by resident staff and volunteers. Although there are outline liturgies which may be used, remarkable creativity is demonstrated. The Warden has overall responsibility for the co-ordination of arrangements and for ensuring that those leading worship are given appropriate guidance. There is a remarkably high level of participation and a high degree too of creativity: as in so many other ways Iona empowers people, gives them opportunities to discover and use talents they may not know they had; in a typical week as many as thirty people may be involved in one way and another; alongside prayers, songs and Scripture readings there may also be, for example, a range of instrumental accompaniment and choral items, drama and dance, readings from poetry and other material.

The Sunday morning Communion service follows more conventional, formal lines, including the preaching of a sermon, and over the summer months especially usually attracts a very large congregation, sometimes out into the cloisters. After the service, reflecting once more the spirituality of connectedness and the integrity of worship, already referred to, those present are invited to share an oatcake with a stranger over a cup of tea in the cloisters, the place of the common life: at one point this was described as 'an old Celtic tradition', but, like the Wild Goose symbol, there are doubts whether it pre-dates George MacLeod, and the wording of the invitation has been adjusted accordingly!

To complete the picture concerning Iona worship, at 2 p.m. every day during the summer months there are also short prayers for peace and justice, focusing on a different topic each day, and geared particularly towards the day visitors who are unable to attend any of the other services. These prayers complement, and often refer to, the displays relating to peace and justice issues, and particular campaigns and bodies with which the Community is associated, that are mounted in the north transept of the Abbey church.

From what has been said already about the integrity of worship and the importance of the rooting of the worship that takes place on Iona in the common life shared by staff and guests, it should be fairly clear that there can be no blueprint of an 'Iona service' in the abstract. The approach is certainly transferable or transportable up to a point, but whole liturgies are recyclable only to a limited extent. While there are some general points that may be applicable, songs and prayers with some kind of Iona Community connection or provenance that may be appropriate, the particular context, setting and circumstances in which worship takes place are always all-important – because it is not about experience in a vacuum; it is holding up to God and reflecting before God on 'real things that happen to real people in the real world' in a very particular time and place.

Nonetheless, because the Community has an approach to worship that is more or less consistent and shows certain constant features which, through a mixture of conscious commitment and experience, would be accepted as natural and standard practice by Members and staff, it is possible to identify some principles on which the Community's worship is based. And it is important to emphasise that these are reflected, as already indicated, not only in how we worship when Members meet together, not only in the daily worship on Iona, not only in the innovative work carried out by the Wild Goose Resource Group, and not only in the liturgical resources produced by Wild Goose Publications. All of these are significant but the principles and approach reach even wider, through the efforts to enliven the worship of their own home congregation undertaken by Community Members and those others who have been influenced by the experience of sharing in worship on Iona, using our material, or attending a Resource Group event. In so doing, the approach reflects the commitment to a spirituality of engagement, recognising that Iona worship is not 'transportable' and that the particularity of the context and situation must be addressed. And neither the Wild Goose Resource Group nor individual Community Members in their own local efforts are alone in basing their activities on these principles. For example, for five years or so three former Abbey musicians have worked as a group called Oran (the Gaelic word for song, also one of Columba's followers after whom St Oran's Chapel on Iona is named) in leading and preparing worship and liturgical workshops at churches, conferences, festivals and other events throughout Britain.

One of the most significant characteristics of the Community's approach to worship is its attempt to be inclusive. Liz Gibson, who has recently become a Community Member following two spells working on Iona as a volunteer, completed a most interesting dissertation on 'The evolution and impact of the worship of the Iona Community, 1938–1998' as part of her theology degree. She says, 'Iona Community worship recognises that different people have different interests and seeks to empower them to realise their individual needs as well as recognising those of others.'

This inclusiveness is evident in several different ways. First of all there is the issue of accessibility, the intention that as many people as possible should feel welcome, reflecting in turn the hospitality and unconditional love of God, that no one should feel marginalised or devalued by the use of language that excludes on account of gender, race, culture or sexual orientation. This is not so easy as it sounds! It is not just a matter of replacing 'mankind' with 'humankind', for example: hymns and songs with exclusive language tend not to be used; there are 'sound' and acceptable collections of good contemporary hymns from around the world; and the version of the Bible in each seat is a modern translation. But the traditional address of God as 'Father' is deeply rooted within the life of the Church, and the Community seeks not only to innovate and experiment but also, in so doing, to incorporate and marry the best of both old and new; so the total replacement of 'Father' with 'Creator' or the occasional balancing use of 'Mother God' is likely neither to be feasible nor to satisfy even the majority, let alone everybody.

The issue of inclusiveness occurs also in relation to the use of words and music, where possible, that are familiar rather than the relics of an alien culture. This is achieved first by aiming to reflect the world-wide identity and vision of the Church, and secondly by trying to ensure so far as possible that the language is that of everyday rather than abstract concepts intelligible only to those with a theological education. This applies to music too: it does not mean that the staple is either 'happy-clappy' choruses or pop tunes to twangy guitar or trendy keyboard accompaniment; there is a readiness to teach and learn attractive new melodies, an imaginative use of solo voices, singing groups, and instrumental skills, and setting new words to well-known tunes of both hymns and folk songs.

In the Community's inclusive approach to worship we are committed above all to relevance and to participation. A very helpful insight into the significance of relevance – not for its own sake, but to bring people to God and to encourage people to listen to and be open to God, and in the sense of what is real and appropriate to the particular context, congregation and circumstances – is provided by John Bell in the introduction to the very first book of Wild Goose songs. But what is said is equally applicable to other aspects of liturgy, for example to the language and structure of prayer.

> The church always needs new songs, not because the Gospel changes, but because the world changes, and God's purposes in the world have to be re-interpreted to become real for the times . . . We live in a country where unemployment plagues and demoralises large sections of our community, and where lochs play host to a nuclear

> arsenal . . . but where are the hymns of protest? . . . Where are the spiritual songs which have clothed themselves in [the] musical richness . . . of a glorious heritage of folk music, of fiddle and pipe tunes, of vocal melodies all in danger of disappearing into oblivion? . . . Where are the words and music which might yet allow those on the fringes of the church, or those who have rejected the trappings of organised religion, to deepen their faith and praise their maker?

And participation in turn is not just about the inclusion in the liturgy of more responses than Presbyterians are accustomed to, or about recognising that the ability to create and lead worship is not limited to those who are ordained or have a degree in theology – although it is of course about both of these things, and the opportunities and encouragement to share responsibility for preparing and leading worship on Iona in particular, reflecting the true meaning of the word 'liturgy' (the work of the people), has already been mentioned. Participation clearly carries with it a high degree of risk-taking: it is much simpler to keep closer control, and it is a tribute both to the commitment and creativity of those concerned that the worship consistently evokes such appreciative comments about its quality and depth. It also involves recognising the contribution that is to be made within the creative process by intuition, life experience, movement and symbol so as to involve all the senses, movement and stillness, sounds and silence.

The extent to which the Community's perspective on spirituality – engaged, connected, integrated – undergirds and permeates our approach to worship has already become inescapably clear. But there are other principles and features which can also be discerned and developed. For example, to recapitulate and draw some of these threads together in a slightly different way, our worship is incarnational, rooted in the belief that God became a human being like us, expressing God's purpose for us all of life in all its fullness, revealing that no part of life is beyond the reach of faith and therefore of worship. This is why worship on Iona seeks to make the connections with everything else that is going on – by involving the people, by reflecting on the shared experiences – but in such a way as not entirely to exclude 'outsiders'. Thus Liz Gibson reflects on the significance of this aspect:

> The bread for the Communion is made in the kitchens of the Abbey and MacLeod Centre. It can be a powerful experience for someone working as a volunteer cook to find that not only can they make meals but their work can create the central focus of worship. It brings the whole congregation closer to understanding the symbolism of the Eucharist.
>
> During the summer of 1997, as part of the Columba celebrations, a crew rowed from Ireland to Iona. On their arrival, just as the Sunday morning service was starting, they walked up the aisle each carrying an oar. The physical effort of rowing was itself an act of worship – by finishing in the Abbey rather than at the jetty they made a powerful statement and included the congregation in their experience. These examples, of bread and oars, are just two ways of symbolically showing how what we do outwith the church walls can enrich worship within.

Our worship is historical, drawing on the Christian heritage and the experience and creativity of our mothers and fathers in the faith, reminding us too that we are part of the world-wide Church. The innovation is, contrary to the perceptions of some, not always about doing completely new things, singing unfamiliar hymns and the like; it is also about marrying the old and the new, blending the familiar and the exploratory in ways that are appropriate to the particular setting and circumstances, and in so doing perhaps recovering and developing understandings which have been around for centuries.

At the same time our worship is provisional, flexible, open to change, shaped by the particular context, bringing together that which is timeless and that which is rooted in specific time and place, exploring the mystery, seeking to express that which is ultimately beyond the reach of words or imagination. The American biblical scholar Walter Brueggemann, in an interview for the US Episcopal journal *The Witness* (April 1998 edition) refers to worship as a tool for social change: 'Praise is the capacity to exuberantly abandon ourselves . . . Praise is really the communal capacity to be foolish, without thought for self. It is the turning of ourselves over to the mystery of God in a public, elemental way.'

On the theme of change, and the contribution of worship to movements for change, alongside the well-known creativity of the Wild Goose Resource Group, deservedly much admired and precious to the Community, the continuing work of those Community Members with special gifts and insights in the field of liturgy is also pushing back the boundaries, seeking to introduce fresh light in relation to less familiar issues and from places farther afield – much as Tom Colvin and Ian Fraser did thirty years or so ago with significant contributions, from Africa on the one hand and basic Christian communities across the world on the other, that still resonate within the life of the Community. Through Wild Goose Publications the Community considers it important to make such liturgical material widely available: the collection *The Pattern of Our Days* contains resources suitable for and used at a range of events – a 'peace liturgy for a wet day'; an act of witness against racism; a series of 'Exodus liturgies' on themes such as exile and promised land; a liturgy for economic justice which starts pantomime-style and moves through reflection on press and other reports to end up with a stark challenge to commitment. Other collections are in the pipeline, similarly drawing together the considerable experience and skill that many Members have in the crafting of liturgies that reflect the spirituality of engagement and spring out of a diversity of local situations; and, as mentioned in an earlier chapter, the influence of the Community's approach and perspectives has spread through the contributions Members have made to other collections and anthologies and through the remarkable extent to which this whole range of material is used throughout the Church, whether at large ecumenical gatherings or in local congregational settings.

Underlying all this, and as part of the inclusiveness, is the ecumenical dimension. Perhaps this scarcely needs further expansion or explicit statement, because it flows naturally from our identity as an ecumenical community, conscious of our heritage and calling as part of the world-wide Church, which carries with it a perpetual challenge to be open, sensitive and creative. But denominational straitjackets still exist and we are frequently questioned about whether a particular service, especially if it challenges, is 'Presbyterian', 'Anglican' or whatever. There is of course no straightforward answer to such questions: some liturgies may be created more or less *ex nihilo*, while others may be composed of material from any number of different sources; there will seldom be a deliberate attempt to stick to or reflect one single denominational tradition; but of course those compiling a liturgy have their own stories and are themselves products of influences and experiences which may be reflected naturally and unconsciously in the process of worship preparation.

Such questions tend to arise especially in relation to Communion services on Iona – both the rather formal Sunday morning occasion, which is in fact closely allied to the mainstream Church of Scotland practice (but with certain significant additions and variations!), and the informal Friday evening occasion which, while thoroughly 'orthodox' in terms of both theology and 'church order', is not really related closely to anything and tends to change from week to week as it seeks to gather up the week's experience, but in ways that can include worshippers who have not been sharing in the life of the islands centres. As for so many throughout the churches the Eucharist may often be regarded as the highpoint and the touchstone of the Community's worship: the issue of sharing Communion across denominational boundaries will be explored more fully in Chapter 10, which deals with the ecumenical dimension more generally. Whenever Communion is celebrated on Iona it is made very clear that all are welcome irrespective of denominational affiliation, indeed even of formal church membership. In the invitation to Communion very often an inclusive form of words is used, such as 'This is not the table of a single denomination, nor of the Iona Community. It is the table of the Lord Jesus Christ which is open to all who love and seek to follow him.' From the reaction that is received, including from many Roman Catholics, it is clear that this eucharistic hospitality is much appreciated.

Within the Community's own life Communion is celebrated frequently when Members meet: it is a regular and important part of the monthly gathering of many Family Groups and is almost invariably included in the programme for Plenary meetings. Although there may not be a common mind within the Community on some of the finer points of sacramental theology, for most Community Members (perhaps even those who belong to the Society of Friends with their different approach to the sacraments!) the celebration of Communion is fundamental and precious, at the heart of our belonging together and our common faith-commitment. In the sharing of Communion are incorporated and encapsulated both the integrity of worship and the spirituality of engagement. Kathy Galloway has said in a paper recently prepared for the World Council of Churches: 'Ultimately for the members of the Iona Community, our worship sustains most, refreshes most, has the greatest integrity, not when our words are most beautiful, our liturgies most reverent or innovative, our music most heavenly, but when our lives are most fully engaged.'

Christ has no body now on earth but yours, no hands but yours, no feet but yours. Yours are the eyes through which Christ's compassion cares for the people of the world; yours are the feet with which Christ is to go about doing good; yours are the hands through which Christ now brings a blessing. (Attributed to St Teresa of Avila)

O Christ, you are within each of us. It is not just the interior of these walls: it is our own inner being you have renewed. We are your temple not made with hands. We are your body. If every wall should crumble, and every church decay, we are your habitation. Nearer are you than breathing, closer than hands and feet. Ours are the eyes with which you, in the mystery, look out in compassion on the world. Yet we bless you for this place, for your directing of us, your redeeming of us, and your indwelling. Take us outside, Lord, outside holiness, out to where soldiers curse and nations clash at the crossroads of the world. So shall this building continue to be justified. We ask it for your own name's sake. Amen. (George MacLeod, from the prayer used in the Morning Service on Thursdays in Iona Abbey)

8

The Development of Personal Spirituality

Spirituality itself needs to be demystified! It has become ambiguous and confusing, esoteric and precious. It has to be rehabilitated from the connotations of dilettantism and religious tourism that it carries in some quarters and rediscovered as a concept that is fundamental to our humanity and morally neutral. Thus spirituality is common to us all, but there can be good and bad kinds of spirituality, approaches that can be healthy and others that can be damaging, some that can be approved of, others that seem undesirable and open to serious criticism. The biblical promise that 'all things will be made new' is not about another world but this one, and when Paul speaks about 'new life' he is talking about the renewal and transformation, by the Spirit of God through and in Jesus Christ, of this life given to us by God. When one hears someone described as 'a very spiritual person' what image is conjured up? Does it, for example, refer to a kind of self-conscious, even self-advertising 'holiness', a tendency, as it were, to wear one's religious heart on one's sleeve, an inclination to name-drop about God, an above-average disposition to talk about and engage in prayer? These may well be outward manifestations of an inner state; but, to pursue the line of thinking developed earlier, and if spirituality is about connectedness, wholeness, energy, engagement and commitment, it is likely to be reflected in style, quality and orientation of life rather than in words alone: it is essentially a matter of being and doing, consistency and authenticity, rather than talking!

Similarly it is a common mistake to separate the functional from the spiritual, to suggest that one thing rather than another is a 'spiritual' issue. This is to compartmentalise life in a way that is ultimately alien to the Gospel – because, as we have tried to show, or at least within the Iona Community's understanding, *everything* is spiritual: God is in the midst of every situation. As a former civil servant I sometimes say, to some of the free spirits within the Community who sit rather lightly to structures and processes, that God can work through committees – and I believe it! So even the most mundane, routine task and experience has momentous potential. But we need to develop the capacity for discernment, for sifting, discriminating and balancing, through which is enhanced the ability to realise the potential.

Ian Fraser, mentioned before as one of the Community's longest-standing members, with a vast experience of ecumenical work at all levels, both through the structures of the churches and through work among basic Christian communities all over the world (see for example his book *Strange Fire*, a collection of stories, reflections and prayers), shares his insights regularly with the Community through a series of Bible studies or 'probes' on contemporary issues in the Community's magazine, *Coracle*, that reflect the scope and the depth of the Community's approach to spirituality. He asserts the central significance of this gift of discernment to spirituality, involving research (the need to be 'serious about God's developing creation and what faces us in the slice of time and space entrusted to us'), prayer ('the mind of the Spirit must be strenuously and quietly sought'), selection (the identification of priorities in the light of the research and prayer), timing ('Jesus was timed through his mission like a boxer from his corner: "suss out the situation"; "get in some telling blows"; "husband your strength"; "in for the kill" – flailing fists every round are not on!'), and 'alongsideness' ('for poor people confused and fearful, acting as a friend is a sign of awareness').

In pursuing an approach to spirituality that emphasises the importance of engagement, being earthed in reality, there is obviously a danger, to which activists are probably particularly prone, of losing sight of the personal dimension, the need for solitude and withdrawal, the opportunity for reflective contemplation that enhances the ability to engage. But, as Thomas Merton, the Trappist monk whose writings have brought inspiration to so many, has said in *Love and Living*, 'Solitude is not withdrawal from ordinary life. It is not apart from, above, "better than" ordinary life; on the contrary, solitude is the very ground of ordinary life.' The two aspects are thus necessary complementary parts of a single process. This is quite clear whether we look to the gospel accounts of Jesus's life, which show again and again that at key times, usually prior to an especially demanding situation, he, and the disciples too, withdrew for an extended period of prayer and reflection, or whether, within the specific context of Iona, we consider the function of the Hermit's Cell within the Celtic monastic life. The mistake is to suggest that one can stand without the other. Sometimes worship on Iona is introduced with an invitation to keep silence in preparation for worship; occasionally there is a variant on the lines 'Let us prepare to meet with God', which tends to convey the impression, misleadingly I believe, that it is *only* in worship, or in silence that we shall meet with God. But to over-spiritualise silence like this is to devalue the significance of so much else in life. Nonetheless, particularly amid busy and hectic lives there is need for us all to discover and experience the value of stillness. 'Nothing is as moving as stillness', as Yvonne Morland has said recently: Yvonne is an Associate Member of the Community, now secretary of Commonweal, an organisation, resourcing the Scottish churches working for justice, with which the Community has had close links for a long time.

There are immensely valuable lessons to be learned from other faiths in relation to the practice of spirituality – for instance from the Buddhist emphasis on interconnectedness (recognising the significance both of the links that ground spirituality in social and ecological ethical issues, and of the belonging together in 'the bundle of life'); from its 'insight meditation' (*Vipassana*, which stresses the gift of silence and stillness, and letting go of concerns and prejudices – a kind of *de*-centring prayer) and from its teaching about the provisionality of all worldly concerns and concepts.

Similarly there is much common ground with Gandhi's more eclectic but distinctive approach to spirituality, his emphasis on non-violence, *satyagraha* or truth-force, and the communal dimension. Gandhi was quite clear that individuals cannot gain or deepen their spirituality while those around are suffering materially; and he believed that the spiritual law expresses itself only through the ordinary, basic activities of life. From even the most superficial understanding of the approach to spirituality and mysticism within the world's other great religions, it is quite obvious that there is nothing exclusively Christian about a spirituality that focuses on the idea of the subordination and abandonment of self, both in terms of appreciating the connectedness of the individual with others and the world around, and in the sense of letting go and being healed of those influences that harm us and hold us back from being 'all-together' within ourselves, and as such, in closer relationship with God.

The Christian approach to spirituality does however add another specific ingredient in the form of a personal faith-commitment. This is a difficult area, of which space precludes anything more than the briefest comment. The difficulty arises partly from the range of theological standpoints and denominational perspectives that exist within the Christian tradition and the life of the Church today, and partly thus from the temptation (which, it hardly needs saying, it is necessary to resist), whether from within Christianity or as between Christianity and other faiths, to assert that one approach is superior to another. For some, faith-commitment is represented by a once-and-for-all definable event involving the acceptance of Jesus as personal Lord and Saviour. For others the commitment may be impossible to locate in time and place but it will be no less steadfast and sincere; there may be more sense of undertaking a pilgrim journey in the footsteps of Jesus, less sense of 'having arrived' than in the former case, and, while the ultimate goals and travelling priorities may be fairly clear, precisely how to get there may be less certain. For the Iona Community this faith-commitment is embodied in the Community's five-fold Rule, which brings together the personal and the corporate, and for the keeping of which, as Chapter 4 discussed, Members are accountable to one another within their local Family Groups.

Through sincere commitment to Christ, worked out in our personal values and priorities as much as in our private devotions, we experience God's transfiguring presence, new possibilities open up, we come alive in surprising ways, we experience, however fleetingly, tantalisingly, the fullness of life which is our destiny within the divine providence and the deepest desire of our inmost hearts. And of course this has a corporate dimension also – the extent to which the life of, for example, the Iona Community may be enhanced or to which, as explained in Chapter 11, our church may be transformed too if it will only be ready to lose its life in order to discover it, to abandon its inward-turned preoccupation with survival in a readiness to take risks, reach outwards in mission that is more than a covert recruitment drive, move forward in imaginative new directions in response to the promptings and call of God. And the spirituality of interconnectedness means that our society, our world too, needs to hear incessantly this transfiguring message, to take to heart the vision of an upside-down kingdom that challenges and stands on their head so many of the dominant values of our day, that takes justice and peacemaking seriously, that in the current political situation within Britain continues to expose from a standpoint well described as Utopian realism the deficiencies of the enterprise culture and the stakeholder society alike, that seeks to speak out against and remedy all the signs of social exclusion, moral disintegration and confusion over civic responsibility.

The essence of the Gospel message of hope, in which any approach to spirituality must be grounded and to which personal devotional discipline must relate, demands the recognition and taking into our lives of themes that resonate with a sense of mystery and miracle, surprise and struggle. We must acknowledge that our individual pilgrimage is caught up in a much wider dynamic, that nothing worthwhile is achieved without a cost, and that the development of personal spirituality cannot be achieved without the kind of engagement that involves 'embracing the pain'. The words of Allan Boesak, the former South African resistance leader and minister, are full of insight and challenge, and poignancy too perhaps, in the light of his own frailty: 'We will go before God to be judged, and God will ask us, "Where are your wounds?" And we will say, "We have no wounds." And God will ask, "Was nothing worth fighting for?" ' There is a very real danger that this most challenging note of laying one's life on the line may be lost sight of in approaches to the development of personal spirituality that are unduly self-absorbed and negligent of the realities round about: 'sooner or later, if we follow Christ we have to risk everything in order to gain everything. We have to gamble on the invisible and risk all that we can see and taste and feel. But we know the risk is worth it, because there is nothing more insecure than the transient world.' (Thomas Merton, *Thoughts in Solitude*)

'Not long ago there were people who were social advocates and others who were contemplatives. Some acted, some prayed. Today these two activities tend to take place in the same body . . . With increasing frequency, people are accepting, as the central theological task of our epoch, the integration of action and contemplation' (Walter Wink, *Engaging the Powers*). The Benedictines on Iona were aware of this eight centuries ago! On the side of one of the windows in the chancel of the Abbey church are carved a cat and a monkey, symbolising respectively contemplation and action, both necessary to a life of spirituality and commitment. Thomas Merton, whose reflections were so rooted in and related to contemporary issues and realities, said,

> The supposed 'inner life' may actually be nothing but a brave and absurd attempt to evade reality altogether . . . Very often the inertia and repugnance which characterise the so-called 'spiritual life' of many Christians could perhaps be cured by a simple respect for the concrete realities of everyday life . . . Meditation has no point and no reality unless it is firmly rooted in life. (*Contemplative Prayer*)

The development of a personal devotional discipline provides the bedrock of the committed Christian life. As Iona Community Members know well from personal experience, struggling within their own situations to fulfil the demands of the Community's Rule, it is not easy, in busy lives that frequently involve family commitments and irregular working patterns to find sufficient time for what Dietrich Bonhoeffer called 'the arcane discipline, deliberate and reflective, being still'. And yet each of us also is aware that our lives are diminished if we do not do so. It need not be the same time each day, although for some of us that will be the best arrangement. We are likely to need to experiment to find out what is most helpful to us, and this may change through time: with increasing familiarity what was once immensely enriching may become a sterile routine, and a degree of creativity and flexibility may be necessary – by using devotional literature alongside biblical study guides, by altering place and posture, by focusing on symbols or visual aids, by adopting particular approaches to scriptural reflection, such as the Benedictine *lectio divina*, and to prayer, and so on.

And it is not just a matter of giving ourselves the chance to 'listen to what God is saying to us'. I am afraid that I am rather sceptical about the kind of approach that tends to suggest that this is the be-all and end-all of personal spirituality. On Iona, as already mentioned, the regular Sunday evening 'quiet time' at the Abbey follows a different pattern from the other evening services through the week, deliberately allowing guests, staff and visitors space for reflection at the start of the week, closing the day which has started with the crowded Communion service whose shape and liturgy is along fairly traditional lines and familiar to most of those attending whatever their denominational affiliation. In the introduction to the service, as those present are encouraged to use the silence effectively and creatively, it is also made clear that, while it is important to take time to stand back from the busy-ness that dominates most of our lives, it is not only at such moments as these that God is to be encountered and heard, for God is also 'in the midst' of life's ordinariness, the struggles, tensions, relationships we experience every day. An integrated spirituality that values the social dimension appropriately recognises that we encounter and 'hear' God also in and through relationships, through our interaction with others, their advice and insights. While stillness and quietness are essential, and the sense in which solitary contemplation involves exploring our inner depths and 'opening ourselves to God' is important, what we describe as the 'voice of God' may be no more than the process of auto-suggestion at work, and what God is telling us to do may very conveniently correspond to what we want to do ourselves for whatever reason. God works in surprising and mysterious ways. This is why it is necessary to recognise that we must be ready to discern the voice and leading of God in all sorts of places and processes, not least in testing our understanding in discussion with others. Australian aboriginal spirituality emphasises the idea of *dadirri* – a kind of alert inner waiting, involving both stillness and openness to the other, the reality of God not only in the depths of our own inner being, but in the engagement and exchange that is involved in human relationships.

The Irish writer Donal Dorr, in his book *Integral Spirituality* (a marvellous compendium of resource material and helpful exercises as well as a stimulating analysis and exploration of spirituality), says: 'From a personal point of view, my spirituality is that which from within me and beyond me calls me to be more authentically human, more fully all that God has destined me to be.' But alongside this he emphasises the aspect of spirituality that is 'a set of attitudes to the world' and adds, 'If we develop a healthy spirituality it is bound to have two dimensions: a living relationship with the God who comes close to us, and a practical earthly commitment to human liberation in one form or another.' So he summarises his views by saying, 'Structural justice, interpersonal respect, and personal integrity all come together at the heart of an integrated spirituality. The area where they meet may be called "Shalom", the biblical word which means all-embracing peace in every sphere of life.'

In reflecting on this kind of integrated approach to personal spirituality, I keep coming back to the familiar verses from the prophet Micah, pointing towards what God requires from those who seek to follow in God's way: 'God has told us what is good. What he requires of us is this: to do what is just, to show constant love, and to live in humble fellowship with our God' – or 'to do justice, love mercy [or kindness] and to walk humbly with God.' This takes us straight to the heart of the nature of spirituality, not just an attitude, not just about the state of our soul, heart, or mind, but issuing and expressed in action – in terms of our believing, our belonging, and our behaving, all bound together in an integrated whole, a life that its best through the grace of God, is consistent, rounded, rooted and authentic.

I have three little mementos from visits overseas that I associate always with this Micah text and give an imaginative depth to its potency. For believing, the call to walk humbly with God, it is a small wooden carving from Lithuania called there 'Dreamer Christ' seen familiarly throughout that country in homes, at roadsides, in books and pictures, sometimes in other most unexpected places. It is the precious and proud national image of a people who have suffered much down the years, but whose faith has stood firm. This image of the 'Dreamer Christ', wearing the crown of thorns, contemplative, at the same time sad-eyed but far-sighted, speaks of the God who identifies with the struggles of the people, the God who in Christ points beyond whatever immediate difficulties or form of adversity surrounds us, who gives us the sure hope of a brighter tomorrow, the vision of a fullness of the life of the kingdom of God to strive for and aspire to. Believing does not mean knowing or understanding all the answers; it does not mean having no doubts; it does mean knowing enough to want to know and experience more; above all it means trusting in the love and promises of God, it means seeking to walk humbly with God, it means following in the way of Jesus Christ. As is said by Gerard Hughes, who has led several weeks' programmes on Iona, in his latest book *God, Where Are You?*,

> Faith is entrusting ourselves to this mystery in which we are living, trusting that love is at the heart of it, so that it is safe to explore, unsafe to rest in what we consider our present certainties . . . Nothing so masks the face of God as our security in our own certainties. With faith in God

we see everything as provisional, and we are always open to new possibilities.

And alongside the believing is the belonging, the call to love kindness, or, perhaps more familiarly, 'mercy' in the Old Testament version, which has to do with our relationships with others. My memento here comes from Guatemala, a country where natural beauty and political tension march hand in hand. It is a little cloth tortoise, blue, red and white, and with its striking vivid colours it speaks out boldly of God's faithful love, extravagant and constant. It speaks to me too of the virtues of perseverance, persistence, and patience – and, in the particular context of our relations with others, of the call to us, inexorable and incessant, not only to love those around us within our family, our own immediate locality or circle of friends, or within the Church as household of faith, but also, at a personal level, to be persistent witnesses in reaching out to share God's love. We are called to extend, in terms of the life of our local churches, the horizons of communal responsibility through serving with reliability, hospitality and integrity the needs of the parish and through working alongside other groups committed to the well-being of the people in our area.

We are called in addition to recognise that we have an identity as not only part of the world-wide Church, which is a strong Iona Community theme, embodied in our overseas membership, our visitors and staff from other countries, and many of our liturgical practices, but also from our sharing in a global humanity with a concern and responsibility that has no limits, geographically or otherwise. In today's world so many trends are working together to erode our sense of belonging together: all the so-called labour-saving gadgets and developments in technology and apparently self-sufficient forms of entertainment that give us an illusion of independence; the increased mobility and possibilities of travelling that make us less aware of the place where we are and less dependent on those around us. There is a pressing need to recover a sense of neighbourly concern; the call to love kindness, to acknowledge the basic human need for belonging, is insistent.

And thirdly in the Micah text, behaving – the call to act justly. Sometimes the Church seems too interested in people's behaving, to be unduly moralistic and judgmental, to seek to prescribe a series of 'thou shalt nots' that are aimed to prevent people enjoying themselves. But, despite what may be the prevailing popular perception, the Christian faith is not about moral straitjackets. The New Testament accounts of the life of Jesus and the teaching of Paul make it very clear that the whole point of the Incarnation had to do with liberation, not only from sin but also from the constraints and limitations of the law, with which is contrasted the extravagance of God's grace. The Gospels show that Jesus was no kill-joy, liked having a party, and wanted other people to be happy, in a genuine, deep-down contented way. Nonetheless it would be wrong to say that behaving does not matter, that 'we can love God and do what we like'. The parental injunction to 'do as I say, not as I do' lacks the authenticity to make it credible or effective, whether related to smoking, drinking, or the belief that sending children to Sunday School while the parents stay at home will turn the former into exemplary citizens or regular church-goers! The language of action is more powerful than the language of words; so the commitment to act justly or 'do justice' is fundamental to Christian discipleship, an imperative of our calling, neither an appropriate nor an optional extra.

The overseas memento for behaving is a little boomerang, brought back from Australia. It is a small replica, attractively decorated with beads, rather than the real thing. On the few occasions when I have tried it out I have not succeeded in getting it to come back to me – and indeed from childhood days I can remember having a real boomerang in our house; I could not make it come back either: maybe the technique has been lacking! But the boomerang reminds us that, within the providence and purpose of God, within the reality of our own experience, we reap the consequences of how we behave, our actions come home to roost, as it were; invariably and eventually our sins of omission and commission catch us up, whether corporately or personally, just as our 'little unremembered acts of kindness and of love' often yield unexpected benefits and joys.

To return for a moment to the tortoise – because I believe there are insights here into the development of personal spirituality – I have a collection of tortoises from all over the world, of many different sizes and substances; some I have brought back from overseas visits, others have been given to me by our daughter and two sons on their return from study, work or holidays abroad. I am certain that the attraction I find in tortoises has a strong spiritual dimension. A couple of years ago one of the questions in a questionnaire that I received through the post asked me to write my own epitaph. I did not read the small print carefully and failed to realise that my answers would be published. So without much thought, and rather to my subsequent embarrassment, I wrote, 'he could not make up his mind whether to be a grasshopper or a tortoise'!

On the one hand there is the grasshopper, leaping around energetically in different directions, settling nowhere for very long, making a good deal of noise at times, and on the other the tortoise plodding on steadfastly and deliberately, sensibly taking time out to sleep, reliably getting there in the end. I suspect I am really a tortoise but would like to have a bit more of the grasshopper in me; maybe a healthy personality, with an integrated spirituality, would have a good balance of both – perhaps with something of the lion and the lamb, the serpent and the dove too, in good measure!

It is of course ultimately a matter of balance. To see spirituality in terms of engagement – with God, with one's inner self, with other people, with the issues of life – over against the tendency, too frequent in contemporary culture, to see spirituality as escape, essentially about self-fulfilment apart from concern with others and the world about us, is not in any sense to diminish the significance either of a regular personal devotional discipline or of the importance, within our own lives, of withdrawing occasionally from the busy-ness and demands of people and situations around us for solitary reflection. Such periods deepen our insights, recharge our batteries, help us, in the words of Richard of Chichester's famous prayer, to know God more clearly, love God more dearly, follow God more nearly. Indeed one of our Community Members, Lynda Wright, runs a retreat house, in Falkland in Fife, which many Members and others connected with the Community find a splendid place to visit for precisely these purposes. The lack of balance occurs when spirituality is regarded as nothing but prayer and contemplation. The location of the Lipchitz statue of the Incarnation provides a salutary reminder that God is in the midst of the everyday, among the ordinary routines and relationships of our lives. The Hermit's Cell on Iona, the circle of stones believed to be the remains of a monastic retreat, has to be balanced alongside the Abbey cloisters, the place of the common life: both had their place within the lives of our Iona forebears.

While, as has been said already, the Iona Community has not deliberately set out to emulate, recreate or even reflect within its life and activities the patterns or priorities of the Celtic Church (which, as indicated above, was much less monolithic and homogeneous than some of today's romantics would wish to believe), it is interesting to trace, as for instance Ian Bradley does in *The Celtic Way* and *Columba: Pilgrim and Penitent*, the extent to which some of the dominant characteristics of the Celtic tradition are reflected in the interaction between the common life and the place that is accorded to the development of personal spirituality. Ian Bradley, with a fine flair for alliteration, focuses on nine words starting with 'p', but in relation to personal spirituality it is perhaps sufficient here to mention only three of these which draw together and sum up so many of the strands and elements that have been mentioned already: first, Poetry – the creative, imaginative side of spirituality, yielding fresh insights and new thinking, the strong hope and sense of vision relating to the purposes of God and promise of the kingdom, striving toward the just, compassionate order of things that those with faith-commitment are called to help bring into being, responding to the signs of the breaking through of God's kingdom; next, Presence – the down-to-earthness of God, the relevance of faith and thus spirituality to every aspect of life, the immanence and immediacy of God, in the ordinary things and places of life as much as in religious observance and rituals; and third, Pilgrimage – moving forward and onward, our personal journey of faith and life but in companionship and connection with others, the intrinsic open-endedness of it all, a degree of flexibility and humility (the state of never quite arriving, 'your God is too small', etc.), and the readiness to be surprised by and respond to the unexpected.

The burgeoning interest in the development of personal spirituality is a contemporary reality which the Iona Community recognises, and indeed would wish to welcome and encourage as relating to fundamental issues of identity, belonging and values that are significant to us all. But the Community, in its integrated understanding of spirituality, and in its affirmation of the importance of engagement, would also say that these issues can ultimately be explored, worked out, expressed only in community, moreover in a life rooted in and underpinned by prayer, both individual and corporate, and worship.

It is certainly true, as Esther de Waal says in *A World made Whole*, that

> numbers of men and women, lay people in the world no less than members of religious orders, are increasingly

> recognising the urgent need to find a place and time to withdraw; that unless we learn to live with ourselves we cannot live with others; that solitude helps towards the fullness of our own humanity . . . Celtic spirituality has always been clear about the role and importance of the solitary life . . . for the underlying principle is that a life of activity in the world is only made possible if it is nourished by times of withdrawal into solitude and silence.

But alongside that it is no coincidence that three of the foremost spiritual gurus of the second half of the twentieth century, Jean Vanier, Thomas Merton and Henri Nouwen, whose works are so popular as sources of spiritual inspiration, all have their roots in Christian community. Indeed the relation between the withdrawal and the engagement, the personal and the corporate provides the structure for one of Henri Nouwen's classic works, *Reaching Out*, as he explores and discusses the insights to be derived from the movement from loneliness (in the sense of being cut off, isolated and separate) to solitude (a deliberate, positive state), from illusion to prayer, from hostility to hospitality towards others. It is this kind of creative, fulfilling process which the Iona Community seeks to reflect and to which we aspire both in our Rule and in the pattern of life on Iona. Predictably, unfortunately, we fall short much of the time. But there are enough uplifting and enhancing experiences, enough intimations of the kingdom and hints of 'glory in the grey' to encourage us to persist – like the tortoise!

> *Bright God of the morning,*
> *summoning the sun*
> *dancing in the wind and the snow and the rain,*
> *You made us*
> *You know us by name*
> *You are here with us now.*
> *Help us to hear your voice*

Within us, among us.
Ground us today in truth and in love.
Strong God of the darkness
Calling us to join the dance
of stars and moons and planets,
For a world where humans try to sleep
And juicy mice rustle through fallen leaves
We give you thanks.
(Ruth Burgess/Obadiah Glimfeather,
Iona, March 1998)

God of strangeness and desire, we bless you for enticing us to the last place we wanted to be, the place where we can hide no longer, where we must face our own emptiness and see our false gods fall. We bless you for the immeasurable relief of self-exposure, for the miracle of survival and for coming to us in unexpected guises. Blessed are you, God of strangeness and desire.

But if we have turned in upon our emptiness, refused the risks you require of us, idolised our self-sufficiency, and clung to our captivity, have mercy upon us, God who wrestles and embraces us. Shatter our illusions, refuse your comfort of angels, feed our hope and our hunger with the adventurous faith of your spirit until grace is our only sufficiency. Amen
(Kathy Galloway, *The Pattern of Our Days*)

9

Political Engagement and the Pursuit of Justice

Kate McIlhagga, a Community member who is a minister of the United Reformed Church in the north-east of England, and for a number of years was joint convener of the Community's working group exploring the rediscovery of spirituality, has described spirituality as 'where prayer and politics meet'. The link between religion and politics, let alone spirituality and politics, is hardly self-evident, although, as mentioned earlier, for many years many people in Scotland, aware of George MacLeod's high-profile campaigning on nuclear disarmament and other issues, felt that the Iona Community was concerned principally about politics and little about religion! And yet, as the theologian Raimundo Pannikar has said, 'religion without politics is irrelevant; politics without religion is dull and uninteresting'.

Against the background of what has gone before it perhaps scarcely needs arguing that a spirituality of engagement demands political involvement, as reflected in the Iona Community's Rule, explored more fully in Chapter 4. Indeed spirituality has been defined by the French

Mission Populaire movement as

> that divine breath that enlivens the coming together of the excluded marginalised people and enables them to stand like an army ready for action. Yes, like an army, a militant people, non-violent of course able to fight against suffering, domination and fear in a word against death. Is this not what Jesus did? He is at the head of this standing army which we have to create. Our spirituality, made of periods of fighting and rest, is a breath that gives us strength to fight death whenever we meet it. It has nothing to do with the apolitical disincarnation of 'extra-terrestrial planners' who do not have their feet on the ground and ignore the reality of everyday life. (Jean-Pierre Cavalie, *Mission Populaire* Newsletter, Spring 1997)

This view, about the inescapability of the political dimension of the Gospel, fortunately appears to be increasingly widely accepted. For too long church and society issues have been regarded as a Cinderella, a kind of optional extra, rather than as central to discipleship. If the Gospel does not have a bearing on every aspect of human life how can it really be good news? And yet a concern for social change, for the renewal of society according to God's purpose is a consistent theme within Scripture and within the tradition of the Church. As Kenneth Leech in *The Sky is Red* has said,

> There is no distinction between the gospel and the vision of a transformed human society. Jesus was far more concerned with the coming of the kingdom of God than he was with the shape of the Christian community in this age. Nevertheless the Christian community, what we call the Church, has a significant role to play as a social organism which seeks to prefigure the shape and form of the Kingdom in which God's justice and compassion will be

manifested in terms of human society . . . The proclamation that God was in Christ reconciling the world to himself, the vision of a transformed society – the Kingdom of God – and the commitment to work with the incarnate, crucified and risen Christ to achieve it, through the power of the Spirit and nourished by word and Eucharist, *is* the gospel. There is no other.

The basic question is 'what kind of society do we want?', raising issues concerning social goals, social values and social priorities, how and for whose benefit limited resources are used. The Iona Community has always approached this from a standpoint of commitment to pursuing social justice, not only in specific activities and involvement in campaigns and issues from time to time, but in a general orientation towards people suffering from social deprivation or disadvantage. This was of the essence of the Community's original life and purpose, not an additional interest. From the early involvement in 'church extension charges' in housing schemes, through the range of activities based in Community House in Clyde Street, the campaigning on particular issues down the years, to the areas of concern identified as priorities and the development of the justice and peace commitment, this has remained central to the understanding of and approach to spirituality, even if it was not always articulated in precisely these terms.

Ultimately this is a theological, even confessional matter, reflecting the conviction that political engagement is intrinsic to Christian discipleship, that the Gospel is good news precisely because of God's involvement in human events in a specific, down-to-earth, embodied way in Jesus Christ and that this is reinforced by an inescapable biblical imperative. The Bible is about revolution as well as revelation, as we are reminded by the old joke about the Greek guide on Patmos whose English was less than perfect. The theme of social justice echoes through the pages of Scripture like an insistent drum-beat - from the

Exodus account of the liberation from Egypt, through the Deuteronomic code with its special concern for the disadvantaged, the consistent, urgent message of the prophets to the life and teaching of Jesus and Paul's pointing to the perpetual challenge of the kingdom of God that stands all worldly values on their head. However marginal an interest in social and political issues may sometimes seem to the mainstream of church life in Britain today, there have been many down the ages who have regarded this as a priority. In the social teaching of the churches, practical projects, and contemporary theological understanding social justice themes have been accorded encouraging significance (from *Faith in the City* to the 1996 statement *The Common Good* by the Roman Catholic Bishops' conference of England and Wales and the ecumenical 1997 report on unemployment, and liberation theology's preferential option for the poor), and this has been a strong concern of the Iona Community from the outset.

Consideration of the theme of social justice on the basis of the cumulative witness of scripture leads inexorably to the conclusion that there is a huge gap between God's purpose for humankind and our world and the reality of life as we know and experience it – giving rise to what has been described, tongue-trippingly, as 'eschatological dissatisfaction' – a deep discontent with the way things are, and an urge to work for change, albeit in the knowledge that the task will not be completed this side of the completion of the kingdom.

Political commitment, a concern for the social order and the world around us is thus bound up with our spirituality, personally and corporately. As I have noted recently, I think from a magazine of the Fellowship of Reconciliation,

> To be peacemakers . . . is to rely in our own weakness on the strength of God. It is to listen for the voice of the Holy Spirit which allows us to see anew the situation we inhabit, the Holy Spirit which shows us what, in existing

> circumstances, must unfailingly be done. It is to realise that justice and peace are legitimately the goals both of the city of God and of the earthly political order, and that our life in religion and our life as citizens complement rather than contradict each other. It is to do work which is neither desperate nor shrill, nor is it a dull and relentless drive towards some narrow ideological end. Rather we will become instruments of the divine creative plan, constantly upbuilding that which folly threatens to dissolve, helping the world's people grow together as a community through the reconciling love of the One in whom all things are one.

Above all the political commitment and concern for social change which the Iona Community's Rule reflects are grounded in Members' understanding of spirituality and the Gospel imperative towards action. Many Members are active in political parties at local level, over the years several have been local government councillors, and several seriously contemplated and pursued the possibility of being candidates for the Scottish Parliament. Other Members are involved, whether as office-bearers or 'foot-soldiers', in a whole range of groups campaigning on particular issues (Church Action on Poverty, Action for Southern Africa, Trident Ploughshares 2000, Campaign against the Arms Trade, etc.), while for many their commitment may be expressed through working priorities, life-style choices, or church involvement in social and political issues at both local and national level. The preamble to the Rule itself says, 'Our act of commitment on justice and peace is "a point of departure". It will remain no more than a pious hope (and a false witness) unless we seek, separately and together, to put it into practice.' Thus the commitment starts from a statement of belief: 'We believe: 1. that the Gospel commands us to seek peace founded on justice and that costly reconciliation is at the heart of the Gospel; 2. that work for justice, peace and an equitable society is a matter of extreme urgency . . .' And it then proceeds to a commitment to action: 'As members and Family Groups we will: 8. engage in forms of political witness and action, prayerfully and thoughtfully, to promote just and peaceful social, political and economic structures . . .'

We come back to the insistent question, prompted by the conviction that spirituality has public significance and is not merely a private matter – What kind of society do we want, can we help to create? How can our vision become a reality? We may fortunately have been delivered from John Major's quaint and banal vision (which went down a bundle in Scotland of course!) of a society at ease with itself, old maids cycling to evensong through the mist while old men supped ale watching cricket on the village green. There was the brief vision of a stakeholder society, almost like a prophetic cry in the wilderness, fleetingly embraced by New Labour in a diluted form that aroused suspicions as to whether this was no more than the discredited enterprise culture masquerading under a more attractive name. The substantial report of John Smith's social justice commission appears to have sunk without trace, superseded by the debate about the future of welfare and in particular by the promotion of the so-called New Deal, with its focus on 'Welfare to Work'.

The debate continues, the Government's package of policies and proposals is gradually unfolded; but there is disturbing evidence that the approach is founded on the underlying, grossly over-simplified belief that all welfare is bad and all work tends to be good. Welfare is regarded as benefits which induce a stultifying kind of dependency and cost the government money, not as an inevitable concomitant of solidarity and communal responsibility, integral to the common good of society, involving indeed, in mutual caring, a highly respectable form of work. And work is intrinsically good, even at its hardest and most boring and soul-destroying, not only because it conveys a sense of personal dignity, responsibility and creativity but also as an activity that produces money. It remains to be seen, for all the encouraging noises accompanying its launch and early days, how effective the 'New Deal' is in meeting its objectives; and there is already concern at the lack of worthwhile and lasting jobs for those who have completed the training programmes. Meanwhile the five giants identified by Beveridge when the Welfare State was created still stalk the land, if in slightly different guises – no longer want, ignorance, squalor, idleness and disease perhaps, but instead the poverty that afflicts at least 30 per cent of our society, the disruptive pressures on the education system, schools and universities alike, environmental pollution, the demoralising effects of unemployment, and all the concerns about health and social services. Can the principle of a service that is free and accessible at the point of need be recovered and sustained in the face of the demands of an ageing population?

These are huge questions which raise major social policy issues; but they are also about human suffering and the lives of individuals in the most immediate and down-to-earth way, and as such are essentially spiritual questions which have to do with basic values and priorities. It is above all in the interaction of the particular and the general, the principle and its practical expression and outworking that the significance of justice and peace in society comes alive and demands something more substantial and authentic than merely an intellectual response. Hence the Iona Community is involved in such matters at different levels and a variety of ways – through what Members do in their local situations, through their churches and through campaigning groups to which they belong; through initiatives taken by the Community corporately and centrally, often in coalition or alliance with other church-related or secular groups pursuing similar goals; through programmes, displays and services on Iona; through consultations and discussions, in working groups and plenaries, often leading to concerted action.

Alongside justice and peace there are two other principles that have important spiritual currency – community and equality. Indeed there is a suggestion that community, as a value or priority, should be regarded as a Christian absolute – perhaps even more highly than love; and that social justice as a value or objective has significance only insofar as it flows from or contributes to the creation and building of community. Clearly community, justice, equality and love are bound up with and fundamental to the purposes of God, however much debate there may be about their precise relation. One of the difficulties is striking the balance between the needs of the individual and the wider well-being of the community to which the individual belongs. Even the New Right ideology at its most extreme (notwithstanding Mrs Thatcher's statement 'there is no such thing as society', much-quoted out of context) does not deny the importance of the social setting: the disagreements arise around how social needs are to be addressed (for example, the Right's reliance on trickle-down philanthropy against the Left's commitment to public responsibility). Generally, however, there is common ground around the spiritual basis of what is at stake, in terms of the universal human goal of fullness of life and the concept of personal growth in community, the links between our individual well-being and the common good; the understanding that we are diminished as individuals by the deprivation of others; where one suffers we all do; and so on.

Equality too is a notoriously hard concept with which to grapple, and yet wherever social justice is under discussion the issue of equality tends to arise, whether equality of access (in terms, for instance, of the availability of services), equality of achievement (or outcome), or equality of opportunity. R. H. Tawney very effectively exposed the flaws in any approach to social policy that was founded on equality of opportunity when he said that it made no sense to give the same opportunities to tadpoles and race-horses, or something on these lines. And it is a similar fallacy to depend too much on equality of achievement or outcome, unless one is talking of achievement and outcome in such general terms as to be almost meaningless: tadpoles, even when metamorphosed, cannot achieve the same outcomes as race-horses; and to go down this track anyway is to collude once more with the approach to evaluation (so popular these days in the appraisal of performance and review of work) that relies on and seeks to assess quantity rather than quality, that believes, as has been said, that 'if you can't measure it, it doesn't exist'. From a Christian perspective it is equality of worth and equality of respect that are significant – on the basis that all are made in the image of God and, in all sorts of different ways, are capable of achieving and experiencing fullness of life. So action for social justice and political change involves facilitating a process geared towards this objective, whatever may be appropriate in each individual case and set of circumstances; and welfare policy must be sufficiently flexible and sensitive to make this possible.

In this context one inevitably comes back to the spiritual dimension of our belonging together, to the interplay between a concern for spirituality and action for social and political change; and implicit in so much of any discussion is the point mentioned previously about the difficulty of securing any kind of moral consensus in our postmodern, pluralist, pick-and-mix society. If values like community, equality, and justice really have no currency are we reduced to an atavistic scramble for survival? This may be seen as, in another form, the debate about original sin or original blessing, the extent to which we believe, as the Quakers do for instance, that there is something of the light of God in everyone, or, to put it another way, an instinctive moral sense, an impetus towards fairness and compassion for others that exists within each of us in tension with self-interest. But it is surely fundamental to Christian witness and service that the purposes and promises of God embrace the particularities of individual lives and specific situations and contexts. It is in making the connections, in relating our own personal story to the Christian story, the local to the universal, the temporary to the unchanging, that lives are deepened and enhanced, community extended, justice established as the kingdom breaks through into the here and now. Thus spirituality is never to be regarded as an entirely personal matter; so often it has a social significance also, a relevance and valency at a public level. The social vision is enriched and transformed as it is rooted in what has been described as the 'radical one-anotherness of Christian community', strengthened to challenge the dominant consciousness and culture through the mutuality of commitment to each other and to the common task. And integral to this process are shared values and a sense of history, inspired by hope, influenced and informed by God's purposes to the point that the 'justice that rolls down like waters and righteousness like an ever-flowing stream' is not just an appealing image but an objective to be worked for in the immediate reality of our own experience.

There is sometimes a tendency to describe and think about justice in terms of fairness: for example the American philosopher John Rawls, in seeking to equate the two concepts as the reflection of a prevailing moral consensus, apparently means a kind of collective selfishness, the notion that the common good can be achieved by the accumulation of individual enlightened self-interest – Adam Smith's economics translated, as it were, into the field of social policy. But from the Christian perspective this is not good enough: there is a clear distinction between seeking fairness for oneself and seeking it for others (particularly vulnerable, disadvantaged people). If one leaves it here it is too easy to equate justice with a pragmatic getting the best deal possible, almost on the basis of a battle about fairness as to which individual or group's self-interest should prevail. How about instead seeing justice in terms of generosity (a theme which Professors Duncan Forrester and George Newlands, respectively of Edinburgh and Glasgow Universities, have recently been developing and reflecting on to good effect)? Clearly justice as generosity goes beyond the limitations of rights and deserts; but is this not the hard direction in which the Gospel points us? This is true not least of the parable of the workers in the vineyard, with its reminder that God's ways and God's perspective on justice do not necessarily correspond to ours, suggesting that kingdom values tend to challenge those of the world – and certainly any which go no farther than prevailing views and preferences. Justice as generosity obviously involves much more than fairness, opens up a deeper, spiritual dimension: it may carry with it notes of forgiveness and reconciliation; it tends to constrain and act as a brake or counter to selfishness and will give priority to the interests of others; it will involve particular concern for those who may otherwise be marginalised and discriminated against; it seeks to protect the underdog rather than to safeguard vested interests.

Thus approached, justice has more to do with self-sacrifice than self-interest. It has a prophetic quality about it, a real cutting-edge that has the potential to make a difference. The churches have a particular vocation and responsibility to maintain a faithful witness in relation to the political system, to reflect that discontent, referred to earlier, with anything short of the perfect condition of justice and peace, the shalom that is God's purpose for this world. Kenneth Leech has said, again in *The Sky is Red*,

> Utopian vision, the dreaming of dreams, is a necessary part of politics. Of course, it is not enough, but it is still necessary – and practical men and women who ridicule it are on dangerous ground and risk destroying that which gives their own work any real rootedness and

> foundation . . . This world matters because God created it, loves it, has redeemed it in Christ, and seeks to transform it into his likeness. Christian people are called to co-operate with God in his work, and this involves a concern with politics. But it involves also a dissatisfaction with the conventional models of the political.

It is encouraging how, at least over recent years, there has been an expectation that the churches and church-related bodies like the Iona Community should be involved in debates about issues of social policy, goals and priorities. And yet, within the life of the churches, many would maintain that little more than lip-service is paid to the priority of the concern for justice; on the whole, issues of social responsibility, and particularly those which involve campaigning for political change, tend to be regarded as peripheral to the mainstream of church life, for the eccentric, the hyper-enthusiastic or ultra-committed, rather than as of the essence and integral to the Gospel. And where there is a greater degree of interest all too often it stops with ambulance work – the social service projects which are thoroughly worthwhile in themselves but which tend to deal with the symptoms rather than the root causes. It is not enough simply to help people bear burdens, to bind up the wounds, to find funding and volunteers for local schemes, however beneficial and imaginative they may be. It is necessary also to strive to remove the burdens, to prevent the wounds being caused. Of course there are huge difficulties in this kind of area and radically different points of view about the appropriate role of the Church – whether as prophet (it is suggested, wrongly I believe, that only individuals can speak prophetically), prompter (offering a word in season from the wings), presence (too passive for some) or pressure group (with a difference of course, and a distinctive voice).

And there is much discussion among those who are interested in this sort of thing as to how specific the Church can be in commenting on specific issues: it is agreed that the Church must be well informed to carry any weight and credibility but while some assert that the Church should stick to general principles applied to particular areas (the so-called 'middle-axiom approach') others would argue that the urgency of some issues and situations calls for the Church to nail its colours more conclusively to one mast. It is highly likely of course that not all will agree either on the analysis of the ills or on the proposed remedy. Some will criticise commitment as confrontational or divisive; but there are many precedents for understanding Gospel commitment and the way of faithfulness as costly and demanding; it is all too easy to sit on the fence, to fail to see that inactivity is in itself a political stance.

The Iona Community has a consistent track record of political involvement since its early days, most notably perhaps in issues relating to poverty and unemployment, to the dismantling of the Central African Federation (where a number of Community Members were working through the 1960s and 1970s), and to the cause of nuclear disarmament, where, after many years of George MacLeod raising a lonely voice in the wilderness, the Church of Scotland's General Assembly in 1982 accepted the Community's anti-nuclear view and has maintained that ever since.

In this field of political involvement the appropriate Christian standpoint might be described as a kind of Utopian realism, a combination of down-to-earth pragmatism and visionary idealism, the quality broadly of being 'wise as serpents and innocent as doves'. This is how spirituality must be worked out and expressed in the political realm, and it makes sense and will come close to fulfilling its potential only in a communal context. Concerted action is necessary, the creation and development of communities of resistance that, through the quality of their belonging together and their commitment to supporting one another and living out the vision and values of the kingdom, are prepared to continue to challenge injustices and the other inadequacies of the status quo. The objective and the process is about transforming community (a theme explored more fully in Chapter 11) – becoming and being a community that works for change, and thus achieving the transformation of the wider community.

These are the aspirations and lines of thinking that underlie the work and concerns of the Iona Community. Frequently we see the needs so clearly in today's society; we are encouraged by all those who respond positively to what we are doing and seek to share our search for more effective and appropriate ways to integrate spiritual and social concerns; and at the same time we recognise how provisional and precarious all our efforts are, and each day we ask for God's forgiveness in our prayer of confession that our lives and the life of the world are broken by our sin.

For each one of us in our own situations these questions remain, insistent and ultimately inescapable – What kind of society do we want? What can we do? It is in communal settings, through the exchange of reflections, insights and ideas, that we can help one another, in ways that are both challenging and supportive, to plan the road forward, corporately and personally, appropriate to the particular context. It is through shared experiences that we are able to sustain our creativity, to hold fast to the vision of justice and peace, to keep alive the hope, to touch the source of all compassion and justice, to be energised by Christ's light and fire. This is what Mary Grey, the feminist theologian who led a week on Iona in the summer of 1998, was exploring in one of her editorials in the journal *Theology and Ecology* (January 1997) when, in commenting dismissively on the 'smorgasbord of current spiritualities' she spoke of the need for an approach that was based on 'integrating body, mind, and spirit into a relationship with God' that was 'closely woven with the discovery of story and identity – identity as a person and in community' so as to provide 'a powerful tool or resource in the struggle for justice'; and she described this as a 'prophetic liberation spirituality'.

On similar lines Leonardo Boff, the Brazilian liberation theologian, has written about the need for a new dream, the need for a new encounter with God as central meaning of life and history, the need for what he describes as molecular revolutions, the emergence of new groups, communities and organisations with a new consciousness of solidarity with those who are oppressed and excluded by the system. For the Iona Community this is what action for social and political change is all about, rooted in its understanding of and commitment to a spirituality of engagement. It is the breaking through of the new future, the fleeting glimpses of the signs of the kingdom that encourage us to look and work for more.

The ideas of community and solidarity come together in the reality of communities of resistance, and the place of such communities, embodying the values and priorities of the kingdom in a thoroughly counter-cultural way within the life of the Church will be explored more fully in Chapter 11. In relation to the particularly controversial issue of globalisation, for example, Bishop Mar Poulouse of India has said (in Christian Peace Conference information newsletter, November 1997)

> In a situation when the rich powerful nations subjugate the less privileged, and when justice is denied to them, what does Christian obedience mean? The Gospel reminds us that there are times when resistance is a form of Christian obedience . . . Resistance is a legitimate part of Christian life and Christian ethics, and we have no reason to be ashamed of it. Resistance is also a responsibility. It is not rebellion at any price without discrimination, but speaking up in a situation when Christians must speak up, even when it seems, at first glance, that it hurts both the rulers and the ruled. This resistance is not directed

> against them but out of concern for them, to enable positive creative change.

As an illustration and example of the Iona Community's interest in and commitment to this area, Ian Fraser, a long-standing Community member, has used his rich range of experience, for instance in setting up Scottish Churches House, Dunblane as a place of encounter between church and society, in his work both at the World Council of Churches and Selly Oak in developing lay ministry and exploring basic Christian communities world-wide, to reflect on 'a spirituality for resistance':

> I so often hear the concept of spirituality restricted to prayer and the devotional life, [but] it must be related to all the points at which our spirits strive with God's Spirit seeking life for the world. It covers the hearing of cries, the depth and quality of response; capacity for discernment, resilience and availability; concern for the neighbour; and a readiness to muck in. Since the Holy Spirit's concern is for the whole world, the command to be alert and stay awake and help others to be equally watchful lest we be taken off guard when a day of decision comes, is addressed to all . . . Spirituality has to do with wrestling in which the inarticulateness of cries and responses is no barrier, because it is not the capacity to get things sorted out rationally which is decisive, but a fruitful wrestling to live in imaginative obedience to God's will . . . Spirituality concerns the depth, the rooting of our action and reflection . . . has that in it which can deal with blows and setbacks . . . is developed normally in community . . . Through reliance on the Spirit there can come that alertness which allows people to see afar off what consequences stem from present actions or what may come out of the blue disconcertingly, so that vulnerable

human beings may be prepared – and have a chance to stand, not fall.

The emphasis on action is important. Ian Fraser himself put this spirituality 'into action' when he was in the forefront of campaigning against the poll tax, and took his case to the law courts, where he met with considerable sympathy but ultimately lost his case. Scotland was the guinea-pig, much to the dislike of the majority of the people; and there were extended protests in which the Community was prominently involved.

George MacLeod himself had for many years maintained a lonely high-profile opposition to nuclear weapons with the whole-hearted backing of the Community. Largely as a result of this indeed for many years the Community, in the minds of many, was, as mentioned earlier, identified with a left-wing approach to politics, not popular, scarcely even acceptable within the Church, rather than with any kind of spirituality or conventional approach to religion at all!

But over the years this has changed owing to a number of factors - among them the adoption by the Church of Scotland of an anti-nuclear policy in the 1980s, consistently held since then; the general movement leftwards particularly evident in Scotland during the Thatcher years; the developing work of the Community in other areas, most noticeably recently in the renewal of worship and the contribution of the Wild Goose Resource Group to the life of the churches. Now, sixty years on from the Community's foundation, there is a sense almost inevitably of the Community becoming an accepted and familiar part of the landscape, and the challenge in this situation is to find ways of continuing to present the radical cutting-edge of the Gospel in relation to the political and social issues of the day.

By and large the Community has not found this too difficult both through corporate effort and through the work of individual members whether contributing through the churches or through organisations with a focus on a particular issue. Thus, for example, there was significant involvement in the Scottish campaign against the Gulf War and, through the Scottish Constitutional Convention, the Coalition for Scottish Democracy and the Scottish Civic Assembly, in the decade-long movement towards the creation of a Scottish Parliament. Two Community members, Maxwell Craig and then myself were conveners, respectively from 1984 to 1988 and from 1988 to 1992, of the Church of Scotland's Church and Nation Committee, in effect serving as the Kirk's voice on the media on matters of public policy, and both have continued their involvement in the national political arena in different capacities – in Maxwell Craig's case as General Secretary of the ecumenical body Action of Churches Together in Scotland, maintaining the churches' joint interest in political and other fields.

The Community has continued to campaign vigorously against nuclear weapons, with members playing a leading part in a number of significant initiatives. Over recent years, for example, there has been the involvement of Alan Wilkie in the World Court Project, relating to the opinion from the International Court of Justice on the illegality of nuclear weapons, and of Helen Steven and Ellen Moxley in the core group, and several other members in supporting 'affinity groups', for Trident Ploughshares 2000, a non-violent project focused on the 'disarming' of Trident missiles at Faslane, near Glasgow in August 1998. The extent to which such activities reflect and are rooted in the Community's approach to spirituality is to be seen not only in the depth and breadth of the perspective that is brought to bear on the commitment (and in particular a persistence, resilience and buoyant hope in the face of repeated disappointments and setbacks) but also in the recurrent evidence of the significance of worship and prayer, not as optional extras but as essential to sustaining energy and efforts.

Another important recent focus of attention has been racism, to which the Community has given priority and had a working group of experienced and dedicated members for some time under the inspiring leadership of Stanley Hope, a retired civil servant in Lancashire, now well into his eighties, who has spent his retirement working among Muslim communities and campaigning for racial justice. This work culminated in March 1998 in the Community's approving a public statement on racism, calling for the urgent repeal and reform of Britain's immigration and nationality laws on the basis that current policies are, and have been since the 1960s, irrespective of the political complexion of the party in power, fundamentally racist and as such socially divisive and morally unacceptable.

Community members are active also in the field of poverty and welfare reform in a whole range of different ways: through a working group pursuing the Community's concern for 'the cause of the poor and the exploited'; through individual members' involvement in local campaigning and support groups (for example, Molly Harvey co-ordinates the Glasgow-Braendam link, part of the ATD Fourth World network); through alliance with organisations like Church Action on Poverty, currently chaired by a Community member, Erik Cramb, whose full-time job, carrying on the Community's tradition of pioneering within the particular field, is the combined role of Scottish co-ordinator of industrial mission and industrial chaplain on Tayside; and through bodies concerned with world poverty, such as the World Development Movement and Jubilee 2000, which is seeking debt relief for the world's poorest countries and which included many Community Members and Associates among the 60,000 who gathered to join 'arms around the summit' when the G8 world leaders met at Birmingham in May 1998.

Members are active in other fields also through membership of campaigning groups at local or national level – particularly in relation to housing (both through the energetic Scottish

Churches Housing Agency and local projects like 'CATH', combating homelessness in Perth, in which Jean Young has had a prominent role), the control of the arms trade, and environmental issues. One of the most remarkable, but also a typical example of Members' involvement, is Larry Nugent, a doughty campaigner for the rights of disabled people especially, whose activities are not at all limited by his being confined to a wheelchair. He described, in a letter about his activities in 1997, how things had been 'a bit rough politically' over the year:

> I had a flirtation with the Trots at street level, demonstrations and such. I soon realised they were a waste of my good time and went back to Kelvin CLP. I am now the campaigns officer for Anderston/City Centre Labour Party branch. The Benefits Integrity passed me as disabled and, instead of the usual five year term, they have put me on a life-time period, up to the age of 80. It is the first time in my life that I passed an integrity examination. Still hope for me yet! 1998 looks intimidating for the disability movement and all people that need personal financial support from central government and the first confrontation is the lobby of Parliament in March. No doubt you will see me handcuffed to some vehicle. Years ago I had no difficulty in breaking into the jail; now the police will not arrest me for love or money.

Although the Community has never had a Member of Parliament in its membership, it has long had close links with many MPs of different parties, most notably the late and much missed John Smith, a regular holiday visitor to Iona and worshipper in the Abbey, whose grave is in the Reilig Odhrain, burial-place of many kings of Norway and Scotland, and now the local Iona cemetery. Many members pursue their commitment to justice and peace-making through activity in political parties at local level, and over recent years several have been local councillors within the Labour and Scottish National Parties – Colin Groom in Fife, Stuart MacQuarrie in Glasgow then South Lanarkshire, Colin Morton in East Lothian, Andrew Patterson in Wigtown, and Fred Riddell in Nottingham, where he served for many years with distinction as education chairman.

Working for social and political change, especially from a Christian perspective, is a demanding and complex business. At one level there is a continuing debate about theology and methodology. This is both academic and practical: where the place of the Church and society in relation to the State is not what it was, and where it can no longer be so readily assumed as previously that there is a shared core of more-or-less 'Christian' values, how do the theological thinking and the consideration of public policy interact and influence one another, and how do churches and church-related bodies like the Iona Community, with a distinctly Christian purpose and a commitment to social and political engagement, work alongside other groups within the alliances and coalitions that are characteristic of the new developing 'bottom-up' political culture of 'civil society', within which the voluntary sector has a much more significant role to fulfil? As within the life of the Community, as it has reflected on and developed its own working methodology and decision-making structures, an increasing emphasis on the significance of dialogue and process can be perceived so that the experience itself, and the effect that it has on the perspective and insights of the participants, has an intrinsic value and all is not assessed by reference to measurable outcomes or the extent to which predetermined objectives are achieved and hopes realised.

At another level political witness from a Christian standpoint is potentially about banging one's head against a brick wall. There is nothing in the Bible, or even within the history of the Christian tradition that promises success. Nor is this what

Christian hope is about. The Christendom vision was misconceived from the outset and is no more sound a basis for mission or social engagement than it was when the cultural environment was more propitious. An approach which sees the Christian vocation, whether individual or corporate, in terms of the remnant or even prophecy is arguably more true to Scripture, and can clearly be derived from Jesus's teaching in the Sermon on the Mount. The metaphors of salt/leaven and light/'city set on a hill', often taken to relate to different approaches – (internal or external influence, witness by action or word, etc) – have more in common than tends to be acknowledged, since neither envisages the need disappearing; and indeed the possibility of the world becoming salt is neither a logical possibility nor very attractive! And such an approach is reinforced above all by what Paul says in the early chapters of 1 Corinthians about the contrast between worldly and the divine values of 'the upside-down kingdom', where the turning-point has to do with death on a cross, within which prevailing notions of success have no currency.

So, while political witness must have defined objectives, it is not appropriate to assess its value by reference only to the extent to which these objectives have been achieved. Clearly the hope is that they will be – eventually perhaps rather than immediately – but the 'success', from a Christian standpoint, lies in the witness itself, in the experience rather than the outcome, in the recognition also that, within the mystery of God's providence, the cumulative effect of the witness, possibly over many years, may produce surprising results, outpassing even the wildest hopes and imagining. The tiny acorns eventually produce huge oak trees; one person plants, another waters, another reaps the harvest; a stone flung into a pool creates ripples that go wider and wider, ultimately producing waves; the flapping of butterfly wings in south-east Asia, environmental pollution in the Amazon valley affect the atmosphere thousands of miles away; the 43759th snow-flake causes the branch to break; the mighty ocean of God's justice is made up of a myriad of water droplets. So in our political witness, grounded in our faith, with our eyes firmly set on the vision and values of God's kingdom, we are called to be authentic to our convictions, to show integrity, to be faithful rather than successful in a worldly sense. And because there will be many setbacks and disappointments along the way, this requires the Columban gifts, according to one of our much-loved Community prayers, of 'courage, faith and cheerfulness' a recognition of the significance of what Martin Luther King called 'keeping on keeping on', and the tortoise-qualities of persistence and resilience.

One of my favourite old Hollywood films, often shown on television around Christmas, is a James Stewart black-and-white classic, *Mr Smith Goes to Washington.* It is a kind of fairy-tale about a decent man in small-town America, who in the pursuit of honesty and public concern, is precipitated into politics and ends up in Washington, on the threshold of the White House. One memorable line of dialogue has stuck in my mind: 'All good things in the world come from fools with faith.' The distinguished anthropologist, Margaret Mead, put the same thought in a slightly different way that challenges us to commitment, and also reassures us in our continuing quest for social and political change: 'Never doubt that a small group of thoughtful citizens can change the world. Indeed it is the only thing that ever has.'

We take the spirit of Jubilee to be a pre-eminent sign of this Kairos time.
We are frightened by the signs of crisis . . .
Encouraged by the signs of hope . . .
Compelled by the urgency of both.
Thus we commit ourselves to the works of repentance – to reparation, redress, revaluing.
We commit ourselves to enact the Jubilee concretely

In our communities, our institutions, our lives.
We commit ourselves to a continuing quest – an ongoing journey – a form of faith in itself, a sign of freedom, a mark of serious discipleship.
The contours of Jubilee are yet to be defined, but the invitation is clear and the need is great.
In the spirit of community, mindful of truth ever exceeding our knowledge,
Let us covenant to live in a manner
Explicitly informed by the Gospel we proclaim.
Amen

(Kairos USA)

O God, you have set before us a great hope that your kingdom will come on earth, and have taught us to pray for its coming: make us ever ready to thank you for the signs of its dawning, and to pray and work for that perfect day when your will shall be done on earth as it is in heaven. Through Jesus Christ, our Lord. Amen (From *The Iona Community Worship Book*)

10

The Ecumenical Dimension

From the outset the Community has had a strong commitment to the ecumenical movement in terms both of the spirit and the structures. Although most of the early Community Members belonged to the Church of Scotland, the Community's work attracted people also from other traditions and this pattern has continued over the years. Today's Community is drawn from all the main denominations in Britain (and similarly the few Members, all the Associate Members and Friends who live overseas belong to a wide range of churches), but as indicated earlier we do not really count as important, or in many cases even know for sure, what everyone else's denominational affiliation is. Our common commitment to Jesus Christ, as a matter of personal discipleship, the heart of our corporate identity, and the mainspring of our shared values and concerns, transcends all the divisions and straitjackets which church structures too often tend to impose. It is significant that many of the older Members and Associates, at formative periods within their own lives, had considerable experience within the Student Christian Movement through the years, roughly from the 1930s to the early 1960s, when its influence both among younger people and within the international ecumenical movement was at its height. While the SCM still exists and carries out many valuable activities, it does so on a much smaller scale than previously and thus no longer serves to the same extent as a training-ground for young 'ecumaniacs', with the result that, for many young people within the churches (and for many older people too!) denominational loyalties are primary and there may be little awareness of or interest in the wider possibilities opened up by the ecumenical dimension. To that extent the Community's ecumenical commitment is arguably more important today than it has ever been, not least because, as will be explored more fully later, these are critical times for the ecumenical movement, both within Britain and internationally.

Within the oral tradition of the Community there are numerous stories about George MacLeod that concern ecumenism and relations between the denominations. 'Are you a Presbyterian or a Christian?' he was liable to ask, especially in his later years, some unsuspecting person he had just met. Or again, he took great delight in asking 'What is the anagram of "Presbyterian"? Best in prayer. And of "Episcopal"? Pepsi-cola!' And it has been handed down that one of the criticisms levelled at him in the early days related to his perceived leanings towards Roman Catholicism and alleged betrayal of Presbyterianism (counter-balancing presumably in a curious way the other charge of communism, on account of the Community's stance on certain social and political issues!). This criticism was based no doubt on some aspects of the approach to worship – for instance, the inclusion of responses, the celebration of Communion more frequently than was normal within the Church of Scotland, the use of candles, and so on. It is encouraging that today such practices, part of the original tradition of the Protestant Reformation, as advocated by Calvin, Knox and their colleagues, are increasingly becoming part of the accepted approach to worship within local congregations of all denominations and that the Community, through the activities of the Wild Goose Resource Group and in the other ways described in Chapter 7, continues to be in the vanguard of the movement to discover appropriate and relevant ways to worship that combine the best of the rediscovered tradition with an exploratory approach that is ecumenical and eclectic.

The film *Sermon in Stone*, which gives a moving and powerful account of the Community's story from its beginnings until the completion of the rebuilding in 1967, includes shots of great ecumenical services held on particularly important occasions – the completion of the cloisters, the Queen's visit in 1956, the 1400th anniversary of Columba's arrival on Iona in 563 – in which church leaders from many traditions and countries played a part. These were not just celebratory events but also had a deeper meaning, theological and dynamic, picked up by Ian Fraser in referring to 'significant points in the development of the Community's life [when] there had been great ecumenical occasions when representatives of divided churches led worship and partook at one sacramental table providing a sign and promise of the great United Church still to come' (*Living a Countersign*).

With the Community's commitment to an approach to spirituality that is characterised, as the preceding chapters make clear, by engagement and exploration, the ecumenical dimension is inevitable. And within the churches there is an awakening interest, evident at different levels and in a variety of ways, in a distinctively 'ecumenical spirituality' – a pursuit that has more credibility in my view (discussed in Chapter 1) than the fashionable fascination for an approach to Celtic spirituality that is too often a travesty of the authentic tradition of the Celtic Church. There are ecumenical spirituality projects both in Scotland and in Britain: Community Members are involved in both, and fortunately there does seem to be some informal relationship and dialogue across the border!

A recently published World Council of Churches report *A*

Christian Spirituality for Our Times recognises some of the features of ecumenical spirituality that are evident also within the life of the Community as we seek, through the personal and corporate struggles, through the difficulties we encounter both internally and externally, to pursue our concerns for the renewal of Church and society:

> We are convinced that a Christian spirituality for our time has its own value as the struggle between the Holy Spirit and our spirit to incorporate our life in Christ. It is an integrating, converting and missionary experience. It makes us slaves of hope in our fragmented world for which we pray and intercede before God, and which still cries out for justice, peace, community and unity. Christian spirituality is not the vocation only of a few, but an essential dimension of the whole of life and work of the churches and ecumenical councils and bodies. It is fundamental to our quest for ecclesial unity which is itself a process of prayer together as well as of reflection and action together.

And again, emanating from the Council of Churches for Britain and Ireland's project, mentioned earlier, with which the Community is even more closely connected than previously, through one of our Members, Ruth Harvey being its director:

> Ecumenical spirituality expresses the common life shared by Christians in spite of the separation of their churches. The common life is one of discipleship that follows from being baptised into Christ. Spirituality is a systematic way of attending to the presence of God. It aims towards a total response in faith that embraces all relationships with God, with one another and with creation. Ecumenical spirituality develops a prayer life based on the Word of

> God and calls individuals to be ministers of conversion and reconciliation with a great openness and willingness to cross boundaries, in an awareness of God's purposes for the whole of creation. It involves engagement in new ways of praying, listening, interacting, deciding and risking. It operates at the grassroots levels of daily living and attempts to co-operate with the Spirit of God at work in the graced ordinariness of daily living. In recognising the call to holiness in all denominations it works ecumenically with groups and individuals in order to bring about a change in the unjust structures where these are found in everyday life.

Here again there is so much with which the Community can identify, and in particular the connections, already noted, between personal devotional discipline and the wider and broader implications, whether in relation to action for social and political change or to ecumenical commitment. All this is of the essence – the cutting-edge of the spirituality of engagement. And the emphasis on both prayer and relationships is thoroughly salutary. In a recently published collection of sermons (*States of Bliss and Yearning: The Marks and Means of Authentic Christian Spirituality*) John Bell of the Wild Goose Resource Group says, 'Spirituality is the oil which fuels the machinery by which we relate to God, to God's world and to God's people.' The relationships are not always straightforward even – perhaps especially – within a Community! The ecumenical dimension of our life together means that there are sometimes differences in how we see things or are accustomed to do things. For example, I cannot get used to, or prevent myself correcting, the description, used by those accustomed to another tradition, of the magnificent marble Communion table in Iona Abbey as the 'altar'! Because each of us sees things through our own filter that is influenced by our personal stories and journeys, there are inevitably differences of opinion from time to time – whether on the merits of liturgical practices, theological perspectives or the key aspects of some social situation. But we have got used to discussing these issues, and on the whole we are sufficiently tolerant of one another, or sensible enough as to priorities, for such differences not to matter against our shared commitments and objectives.

This is not to underestimate the significance of our differences and our individuality, or to gloss over them either through pretending they do not exist or through some cheap and easy process of reconciliation. On the contrary, as our justice and peace commitment says, 'we believe that *costly* reconciliation is at the heart of the Gospel' and this is equally true of commitment to increasing ecumenical co-operation and to promoting greater ecumenical understanding. There are some things that can be taken for granted and others that have to be grappled with and worked through and sometimes it is not clear into which of these categories a particular issue falls: often they seem to be referred to or land up in the mail-box of the Leader! But over the years we have become accustomed to living creatively with our differences to the point of making an advantage of our diversity and focusing on specific actions and events, so that discussions are grounded in practical reality rather than conducted on an abstract level.

The ecumenical dimension of the Community's life – and of its understanding of spirituality – is to be seen also in the Community's active and enriching links with other ecumenical communities (such as the Corrymeela Community in Northern Ireland, with whom we have a lively and much valued relationship), the ecumenical centres that we use and pray for regularly (such as Scottish Churches House, Dunblane, where there have been strong connections since the beginning, especially when the warden was a Member – Ian Fraser, and then Richard Baxter), ecumenical networks such as the

Association of Laity Centres within Britain and the European Association of Academies and Laity Centres, and with the official ecumenical structures within Britain.

Since 1951 the Community has had a formal relationship with the Church of Scotland. At that time it was decided, as a means of maintaining contact and ensuring satisfactory communication, to create an Iona Community Board, appointed by the Church of Scotland's General Assembly with a further few members elected by the Community. Through this Board the General Assembly each year hears a report on the Community's activities and has an opportunity of offering comments. This is a channel for information rather than a way of exercising control and authority, since the Community as an independent charity and limited liability company has it own directors and executive committee – the Community's Council. In 1993 there was a radical innovation when, at the Community's suggestion, the General Assembly agreed that, to reflect the Community's ecumenical character and commitment, the Board should also include as members in their own right, expenses met by the Church of Scotland, nominees of other denominations with a substantial number of Community Members: this was the first Church of Scotland Committee to be so constituted, and there are members at present from the Quakers, the United Reformed Church and the Church of England, and it is hoped to add a Roman Catholic appointment shortly. And the Community's ecumenical commitment is reflected also in the formal connection we have with the new ecumenical bodies created in Britain in 1990. As a 'body in association' with the Council of Churches for Britain and Ireland, with Action of Churches Together in Scotland, and Churches Together in England the Community has both ready access to a network of contacts and also has increased opportunity to contribute to events and initiatives on a whole range of issues.

Such events and initiatives are an important part of the shaping of tomorrow's Church and of reflecting on the relevance of the Gospel and of spirituality to the times in which we live. Thus spirituality that is ecumenical and engaged takes a variety of forms. Church structures and worship, as commented on above, are two of these. It is equally evident in major ecumenical events in which Community Members and Associates will often be found taking a significant part. Over recent years Members have been prominently involved, for example in the German Kirchentag, the General Assembly of the Council of Churches for Britain and Ireland, the 1997 Scottish Christian Gathering, the Forum of Churches Together in England and the Assembly of the European Ecumenical Commission for Church and Society – whether as organisers, workshop and worship leaders, speakers or participants. In addition to the invitations that Members receive to lead workshops or speak at conferences, both in Britain and overseas, whether arranged ecumenically or within a single denomination, a number of Members have recently served as consultants at World Council of Churches events, most notably Lesley Macdonald (women's issues), Colin McKenzie (inter-faith), John Bell and Kathy Galloway (worship). Several members, moreover, are due to attend the eighth Assembly of the WCC at Harare, Zimbabwe in December 1998, including Gavin Elliot and myself as two of the four Church of Scotland representatives, where it is planned to run workshops in the 'Padare' or market-place on the Community's approach to spirituality.

One of the most significant ecumenical events over the last few years was the second European Ecumenical Assembly held in June 1997 at Graz in Austria under the joint auspices of the Conference of European Churches and the Council of European Roman Catholic Bishops' Conferences. The theme of the Assembly, attended by over three thousand official delegates and visitors, was 'Reconciliation: gift of God, source of new life'. By all accounts the experience was shot through with a sense of both engaged spirituality and the costliness once more of genuine reconciliation. The official delegates got bogged down in the drafting of official resolutions and discovered, in the face of all the tensions within Europe around issues of the enlargement of the European Union and NATO, market pressures and post-Berlin Wall scenarios, that reconciliation and improved ecumenical relationships were very much harder goals to achieve than had been envisaged. From the stimulating and interesting reports given at Community Week 1997 on Iona by the Members who had been there in different capacities it was clear that, as so often, the fringe events had been very much better than the formal sessions and the visitors had had a very much more rewarding and enriching time, with so much more chance to engage and make connections with both issues and people, than the official representatives!

The Community's ecumenical commitment, as much as our concern for social and political change, is a natural outworking of the incarnational theology that sees spirituality as engagement and connectedness. It stems from our understanding of the vision and values of God's kingdom and the imperative to respond positively and play a creative part wherever there are signs of hope and growth, as the kingdom breaks through. If the Church is truly a sign and the first-fruits of the reconciliation of all things in Christ then our divisions represent a betrayal of our nature and calling, and anything other than a strong commitment to unity is to commit the enormity of dismembering the body of our Saviour in terms of the insights and language of the first chapter of the First Letter to the Corinthians.

Within the Community we are working both corporately and in our local situations across the denominational boundaries, often, as has been said, without awareness of the denominational affiliation of our fellow-members or those with whom we are sharing the journey, simply because it does not really matter. We seek to extend and deepen mutual understanding and find ways of co-operating more fully. For some years now, since the 'strategic planning' exercise that included the identification of particular 'areas of concern' as priorities and the creation of working groups to pursue these, a group of members has been focusing particularly on ecumenical issues. The group took as its first priority and name 'sharing Communion by the year 2000'. It held two consultations on Iona, bringing together people with a range of church backgrounds and experience of the issue. And, a little more controversially for some, at the group's instigation, and after discussion in plenary, in 1996 the Community launched a petition with the aim to make possible the sharing of Communion at designated ecumenical centres and events, so that where people are gathered together and share everything else, by way of worship, meals, discussion, informal conversation, relaxation time, they may not be prevented from also sharing at what is for many both the deepest and the highest point of worship. As mentioned already, when Communion on Iona is celebrated in the Abbey on Friday evenings and Sunday mornings, it is made clear each time that the table belongs to Jesus Christ and is open to all those who love and seek to follow him. We were immensely encouraged that the petition, which was circulated through the ecumenical structures, mostly at the grass roots, attracted so much support. It was presented at the Graz Assembly in June 1997 and received much favourable comment and attention. We followed it up with work on the recent Papal document on ecumenical relations *Ut unum sint* (That they may be one), on which a special consultation was held on Iona in the summer of 1997, following which formal messages were exchanged with the Vatican. It is intended to continue to promote discussion of these important issues, because we believe that the more they are considered, and the more experience people get of the common ground they share, across the denominational divisions, the sooner change will come – through an irresistible bottom-up movement rather than a top-down instruction.

We are not blind or naïve about the difficulties in this area. Indeed many of them have surfaced within the Community itself, both around the celebration of the Eucharist in the course of our normal life and around the petition too. On the one hand, some of our more radical Members have said that such a petition is irrelevant and gives much more credence to church structures and authority than they deserve. On the other hand, some of our Roman Catholic Members have felt that the petition was directed particularly at them and their tradition. But we are certainly not saying that the obstacles to fuller ecumenical sharing lie all on one side; in fact they are on all sides in that, for example, Presbyterian ordination is not automatically recognised by the Anglican Communion, although the converse is acceptable, and there are many Protestants who through sectarian prejudice would not wish to share Communion with Roman Catholics anyway. But the reality is that the divisions within the Church today are an incomprehensible mystery to those outside and as such both a barrier to mission and a scandalous blot on our discipleship. Moreover, as most of us know from experience, we frequently find that we have more in common with kindred spirits from another tradition than we have with some members of our own denomination who have a different theological perspective and priorities from ours. A concern for reconciliation and church unity must not be confused with an inexorable process towards uniformity, for living with diversity can be immensely enriching provided there is a spirit of openness and mutual respect. It is possible to be united and yet not uniform, to retain distinctive characteristics. This is already evident within most of the main denominations. It is even evident within the Iona Community!

On St Columba's Day 1998 the Community's ecumenical group (more accurately a network) took the step of proposing a new name for itself ('Called to be One' – also the title of a major project undertaken by Churches Together in England);

and this change was subsequently accepted by the Community. Acknowledging the significance of the work already done and the arrangements for keeping a continuing 'watching brief' on the issue of sharing Communion, the new conveners of the group, both working in ecumenical situations in 'new towns' (Livingston and Telford), said in a letter to Members, 'we feel that there are other equally important aspects of ecumenical work, and that this area of concern needs to tackle them as well'. A two-year programme is planned, with a greater focus on Members' own local involvement in ecumenical ministry and mission and on the sharing of experience and the intention of holding a plenary meeting of the Community in early 2000, possibly in Livingston, Telford or Milton Keynes, to explore such issues further.

The understanding of spirituality as engagement and 'an energising kind of connectedness' permeate a book that the Community published in the summer of 1998, edited by Maxwell Craig, a Member who from 1990, as the first General Secretary of ACTS, was one of those (like Murdoch Mackenzie, who has since 1994 been Ecumenical Moderator in Milton Keynes – an episcopal role and the only such position in Britain) who in a sense embodied the Community's ecumenical commitment. The book is called *For God's Sake – Unity* and contains chapters, by Members and others, from a range of denominational perspectives, from Scotland and England, on different aspects of the ecumenical debate. 'The eight contributors to the book are more like an eightsome reel than a rowing eight. Their contributions are distinctive, expressing their widely varying experience, yet all are committed to the cause of Christian unity. But what kind of unity?' Views and possibilities are explored, in the context of such fields as worship, prayer, education, mission, in relation, for example, to the degree of visibility that unity must have, the difference between the spiritual unity we already have in Christ and a fuller kind of 'organic' unity. The book does not attempt to offer a single simple answer to this question that may be regarded as the Community's 'official line', but is rather intended as a contribution to discussion, especially at local level.

The wider ecumenical context within which the Community pursues these concerns is in something of a state of flux. Neither at local nor at national level have churches demonstrated in the practicalities of their life and activities day by day that they have really taken on board 'the Lund principle' to which they are committed – that churches should no longer do separately what they can do together. As has been noted already, one of the characteristics of postmodern society is that people do not so readily commit themselves to joining organisations which they are expected to support on a regular basis; and where they do join the belonging is pretty localised. So members of congregations tend to relate more closely to what is going on locally than to the structures and activities of their denomination at national or even district (Presbytery or diocese level). And in the same way even local ecumenical projects, let alone the national and international structures and events, tend to be regarded as extraneous – as 'them' rather than a natural part of 'us'. Nonetheless there is encouraging evidence of gradual awakening of increasing interest, at least at the grass roots, as more and more experience is gained of working together, as common ground and shared purposes are discovered, relationships are established and mutual trust develops. The interim proposals produced under the Scottish Churches' Initiative for Union (SCIFU) will no doubt also generate additional interest and discussion that it is to be hoped will continue to help this process and lay a foundation for some modest structural changes that will be beneficial to the life of the churches and their local communities. But at a time when the churches generally are weathering what amounts to a crisis of confidence, ecumenical concerns tend not to rank high on the order of priorities. Exploring this theme in *God, Where*

Are You?, and commenting also on the extent to which ministerial enthusiasms and aversions can affect congregational attitudes, Gerard Hughes says,

> It is because we are divided into our separate denominations and live in clerically dominated churches, and the clergy are so busy trying to keep their own churches going and in coping with the burdens of administrative work, that ecumenical activity is low on their list of priorities, if it has any place at all. Consequently the divisions remain and church membership dwindles.

Inevitably this also affects the ecumenical bodies and structures at many levels: the Council of Churches for Britain and Ireland is emerging from a fairly difficult review process which will be completed at the Assembly to be held in February 1999; the Conference of European Churches, at a particularly demanding time with the emergence of the churches in central and eastern Europe from years of repression under communism, has to contend with serious financial pressures, largely resulting from the reduced contributions from the German and Scandinavian churches with the change in their church-tax arrangements; and the World Council of Churches is bringing to its Jubilee Harare Assembly in December 1998 new proposals for 'a common understanding and vision' and for its own structures and priorities in the light of the challenges presented by the same financial pressures, by the delicacy of relations with its Orthodox members on the one hand and the Roman Catholic Church on the other, by the shifting centre of gravity away from the European and North American which so dominated its early years towards the South, and particularly Africa where churches are still growing rapidly, and by the apparently increased significance of other major international groupings, both confessional (Lutheran, Reformed and Anglican as well as Orthodox) and 'evangelical'.

The theme of the WCC Harare Assembly is 'Turn to God – Rejoice in Hope'. Hope is above all the distinctive Christian characteristic, the hope that is founded on the reality of resurrection and the promise of the kingdom. It is hope that inspires and energises spirituality towards engagement and points beyond the disappointment and discontent. In preparation for the Harare Assembly a theologian from Zimbabwe, Sebastian Bakare has prepared a very helpful book entitled *The Drumbeat of Life*, highlighting the visions and dreams that come from the African experience, the ideals of collaboration and solidarity that are necessary to good ecumenical relations, the importance of genuine dialogue and the sharing of resources:

> The mission of the church today and in the future is to call people to become one forgiven and reconciled jubilee community, in which all members are equal partners, a community without majority and minority, a community of commissioned ambassadors of God, called to proclaim the gospel to all nations . . . 'Turn to God – Rejoice in Hope' is also a call to the renewal of the ecumenical vision. As a community of faith, we turn to a God who is always present, renewing and transforming the church. Ultimately, the ecumenical movement depends on the power of the Holy Spirit for this renewal.

The last section of Bakare's book is headed 'the dance of life and the drumbeat of hope'. There is a strong sense of positive and creative movement, of 'that feeling of connectedness without which the dance will lose its rhythm': within the ecumenical context the spirituality of engagement is about going somewhere!

And similarly, the subtitle of the Community's recent book on ecumenical issues is 'an ecumenical voyage with the Iona Community'. When the Pope came to Scotland some years ago, one of his speeches included a memorably phrased call to walk hand in hand on our continuing journey. Inspired by that vision the Community's spirituality has an ecumenical dimension, carrying with it the call to the kind of 'costly reconciliation' that the Gospel demands. The Greek word used in the New Testament for reconciliation has to do not with compromise, lowest common denominators, finding a tentative way between apparently conflicting opposites. It has to do with new relationships, with 'holding together profoundly different identities in a workable concord, with all its accompanying creativity and disturbance'; it involves transformation, change and exchange so that barriers are broken down, divisions are overcome, something new is created, new possibilities open up. Somehow the worship, once again, sums all this up – the togetherness, the connectedness, the exploration, the engagement of body, mind, and soul, heart and emotions, especially perhaps in Iona Abbey where past, present and future somehow coalesce so mysteriously and powerfully. Here is a deep experience, thoroughly inclusive, transcending denomination and every other kind of boundary, leaping and soaring wonderfully and yet so down to earth, touching lives with joy and hope in ways that are totally new and at the same time so old.

In the reports on Family Group meetings that are circulated to members regularly, one of the groups recently gave an account of a discussion that summed up the ecumenical dimension of the Community's life and some of the principal issues involved. The meeting was hearing about

> the changed focus of the 'Sharing Communion' group. This led to a discussion on the ecumenical nature of the Community. How aware are we? Are we sometimes insensitive in our campaigning for shared Eucharist, as to the position in which we place Roman Catholic members on the one hand and Quaker members on the

other? The question was asked, '*Are* we an ecumenical Community?' We don't feel it necessary to identify ourselves to one another by our denominations. But what is this saying? That denominational levels don't matter? Or that we are denying our differences? Some of us are happy to accept practices when *we* are worshipping together that we would not tolerate within our own traditions. Does all this mean that our Community *is* another denomination, despite all we say?

I think we eventually concluded that it did *not* mean this, but rather that our kind of belonging together transcends denominations – which is what religious communities are all about. The fact that we don't talk about denominationalism much may simply mean that church unity is not our focus. Our focus is to do with justice and peace, community, building, linking prayer and work, etc. Most of us would find a single denomination too narrow a place from which to pursue such purposes. We *are* an ecumenical Community, but our ecumenism is a means rather than an end.

And with that, we said our prayers, and went home!

Christ of the pilgrim path,
and of every pilgrim heart,
thank you for revealing yourself
in situations we would prefer
to pass by.

Christ of the pilgrim path,
you never see us as rich or poor, black or white,
educated or illiterate,
but as one family, involved with each other,
walking together in your Spirit of joy.

Christ of the pilgrim path,
you recognise our many gifts
even when we do not see them ourselves.
may your enabling Spirit free our creativity
in worship and everyday living.
(Peter Millar, *An Iona Prayer Book*)

Gather us or scatter us, O God, according to your will. Build us into one church, a church with open doors and large windows, a church which takes the world seriously, ready to work and to suffer, and even to bleed for it. Amen
(A prayer from the Hungarian Church, (adapted), *The Wee Worship Book*)

11

Where Does the Church Fit in?

This chapter is the book that never was! For seven years or so before being elected Leader of the Community I lectured in the Faculty of Divinity at Glasgow University. How I arrived there is still something of a mystery. It is interesting to look back on one's life and see traces of a shape and pattern that were far from evident at the time. To go back even farther I am aware that, in a way that is much less frequently to be found among young people of today, the Church has always seemed to be a natural part of my life. Going to Sunday school and then to Bible class was a matter of course, and there was no contrary peer group pressure: in a medium-sized Scottish town in the 1950s it was those who did not do so who were the anomalies. Looking back now I see that this amounts to a process of spiritual formation and I am immensely grateful that it was fairly gentle and low-key: I do not recall major battles, Christian commitment was strong and touched every aspect of life, much more than mere Sunday observance, and yet never felt limiting or oppressive. We always had grace at meals but there were no family prayers. The Church was there to attend and support but did not dominate: I did not join the youth fellowship and on leaving home for university, while attending daily prayers and the Sunday chapel service regularly, did not become involved with any of the then-flourishing student Christian societies, but with sport and the running of both the students' union and the hall of residence where I stayed. And yet when a career choice had to be made, the place of the Church and my commitment to it was sufficiently important for me to consider training for the ministry, as my father had done thirty years before. Like him, who became a teacher of classics and then an inspector of schools, I chose otherwise, on the basis of some wise advice, from some people I did not really know very well: looking back now, it does seem part of a process in which God was at work, both reflecting and developing the spirituality of engagement to which I am now so committed; and I still have not worked out an entirely satisfactory theological explanation of it all – how to express this strong sense of the guidance of God, often perceived retrospectively rather than at the time (indeed, as mentioned before, I am rather suspicious when people talk of a sure and certain feeling that God is 'telling' them to do something!), without losing the reality of individual freedom of choice. Bishop David Jenkins has rightly dismissed the idea of a 'laser-beam God', a cosmic puppet-master, impossible to reconcile with the reality of suffering and with God's loving purpose for the world revealed conclusively in Jesus Christ. So I have to accept, despite two honours degrees, much reading, talking and reflecting, the limitations of my understanding against the mystery and greatness of God: God's ways and thoughts are not ours; 'there are more things on heaven and earth than are dreamt of in your philosophy', as I think Hamlet told Horatio!

And yet, as I moved to Edinburgh to work in the civil service there, the Church was an anchor, alongside everything else that I was doing. I became involved in a very imaginative series of projects in the city-centre of Edinburgh, first a three-nights a week beat-club, in a church cellar with a whole range of associated activities, and a little later, moving on from there, a late-night coffee house, also in a church crypt, open only at weekends, for which people of a remarkable diversity of ages and backgrounds queued to get in, because this was the early 1970s, before the pubs and other facilities were open late.

These were life-changing experiences in all sorts of ways, leading to friendships that have lasted (not least my marriage!) and shaping the conviction that, interesting, demanding and rewarding in its own way as my civil service career was turning out to be, I should after all offer myself as a candidate for the Church of Scotland ministry. My wife and I were also very involved in the life of one of the Edinburgh city-centre congregations and I remember the minister, a former Community Member, giving cautionary advice about the potential difficulties, at a personal level, of working for the Church full-time, and the difference between that and the kind of involvement I had had up to that point. This may of course be my memory playing tricks, or what I heard rather than what he said, but I was puzzled, and to some extent still am, at his apparently, yet totally uncharacteristic, compartmentalised line of thinking at this point – an integrated understanding of spirituality as engagement would surely see a Christian's work and witness in a secular setting as itself a form of ministry, God-given, potentially Spirit-inspired in accordance with the Reformed tradition's theology of vocation. The less self-confident part of me still wonders if he was trying to put me off, doubting, perhaps rightly, if I would cope with some of the personally demanding aspects of parish ministry!

It was with the clear intention of being a parish minister that I embarked on the next stage, not only because that is where most job opportunities existed, and still do, within the Church of Scotland, but also because I wanted to continue, if in a slightly different way, my involvement in the kind of missionary outreach to the community that I had already experienced – and the parish seemed the best place and way to do this. But things worked out otherwise and after theological studies and a probationary year in a suburban parish I found myself in university chaplaincy – six very interesting and challenging years, when together with pastoral, liturgical and educational work there were opportunities for community-building, for getting alongside a whole range of staff and students on their own journey of exploration, pursuing questions of meaning, purpose and priorities, and developing my interest, discussed in Chapter 9, in the churches' role in social and political issues. I soon realised that here, in chaplaincy work, every bit as much in parish ministry, was the front-line of mission – representatives of the Church, both lay and ordained, standing beside people in ordinary situations. Here, looking back on it, was where my understanding of the theology and nature of mission broadened and deepened, and I obtained new insights into the significance of spirituality as engagement and energising connectedness. And all this was based too on what had gone before, my experience of the Cephas youth project and the Cornerstone coffee house.

It is both startling and depressing that the lessons learned and insights gained still seem so fresh and relevant. Similarly it is instructive to re-read some of the books and church reports of the late 1960s and early 1970s, hailed as pioneering and revolutionary by some, dismissed by others as insufficiently 'spiritual'. The churches within the Reformed tradition proudly and frequently refer to the familiar maxim – *ecclesia semper reformanda*. But they often mistranslate it, and they too seldom show signs of taking its message to heart – not a Church ever changing, but a Church always needing to be changed! And this is the challenge facing the Church as it looks to the future today, with all the signs of dwindling numbers and declining confidence, a time rightly described as a crisis, with the connotations of judgment that that word carries from its Greek root, for the Church shall surely be judged by its response and bear the consequences of the decisions and choices it makes.

As the South African theologian Allan Boesak has said, 'Remember the church is the chosen people of God. But the chosen shall be known by their choices.' But, as the Japanese word for crisis, made up of two characters depicting danger and opportunity, pointedly reminds us, a crisis is not only a time that may be difficult, even life-threatening, but it also presents an immensely rich opportunity for creative action. And if the Church is to seize this opportunity it must show more readiness to change and be changed than has been evident these past years. It is going to have to overcome the resistance to innovation, exploration and experiment, lay aside the reluctance to take risks, and put behind it the preoccupation with survival that have tended to frustrate progress thus far. It is a natural tendency in adversity to entrench and batten down the hatches, to seek to do the old, familiar things even better. But the cause of the kingdom calls for a different direction from this entirely, the essence of the Gospel and the loving purposes of God have to do with risk, surprise, the doing of a 'new thing', and the insight that fullness of life is to be experienced only through being prepared to give it away.

I first learned some of these lessons in and around Edinburgh's West End, in Cephas and the Cornerstone, and they were reinforced and developed through subsequent experience. These were truly life-transforming, spirituality-shaping years for many people. Horizons were extended in all sorts of ways; people found themselves capable of so much more than they imagined; personal faith grew and its relevance became clear to artistic, social, political and other concerns; the building of community was fundamental, based on mutual trust and an intimate kind of sharing, rooted in worship, crossing all denominational boundaries, inclusive and affirming. Of course many mistakes were made, there were extremely difficult times, hair-raising and sometimes violent situations, alongside all the joys and the laughter.

And, as perhaps it is easier to see now than it was at the

time, the influence of the Community was there, perhaps not always explicitly or obviously, but through some of the people who were involved, whether offering ideas, resources and support in the background or more actively involved in the forefront; and the vision, the sense of purpose, the spirituality that inspired these projects and held them together were broadly in line, perhaps by design, perhaps by accident (and every Community Member is well acquainted with George MacLeod's familiar saying, 'If you think that's a co-incidence you deserve a very dull life'!), with those of the Community.

Over the years my conviction has grown ever stronger about the significance of two aspects of this experience. First, ministry belongs to the whole people of God. This is a view to which the Community has been committed not only in principle (it stems, after all, from the sixteenth-century Reformers) but also in practice for many years, and it was a favourite theme of Ralph Morton, who while Deputy Leader to George MacLeod, wrote, along with Mark Gibbs, two books on the subject that were very popular twenty years or so ago: *God's Frozen People* and *God's Lively People*. Cephas and the Cornerstone were run by a community of lay people: from time to time there were some ministers and priests among them, but they played their part just like everyone else and had in no sense a dominant or leading role. There is a culture of expectation, however, around today's Church that often generates the feeling, even within ministers themselves, especially when everyone seems so very busy, that where responsibilities are shared around, particularly where lay people are involved in the preparation and leading of worship, somehow the ordained person is not doing what she or he is paid for. And yet it is so obvious that one-man (and they usually are men!) bands lead to burn-out, while the involvement of more people increases the task of holding everything together but is so much more interesting, enriching and empowering for all.

The second issue relates to mission, its purpose and theology, its context and strategy. Through the West End experience and my chaplaincy work my interest in this deepened, enhanced also by the results of my becoming more fully engaged with the Community. After all the Community's roots and origins lay in mission, and its continuing purpose – to seek, explore and embody 'new ways to touch the hearts of all' – is fundamentally missionary. Thus it was that my next move was to a lecturing post in Glasgow University's Faculty of Divinity, much to my surprise, as a kind of 'accidental academic', with no post-graduate research experience, indeed lecturing in subjects that I had never formally studied. My field was what is called in the Scottish universities 'practical theology', a misleading title to the extent that the uninitiated tend to think it is all about giving would-be ministers hints and tips how to preach and counsel the bereaved. The courses I developed, however, based on my reflection on experience as much as on my own theological training, had to do with the place of the Church in the modern world – Church and society, Christian ethical issues, modern church history, and especially urban mission.

After six years in the university I was fortunate enough to be allowed two terms' study leave and I embarked on a study of urban mission, extending my reading in this and related areas, and looking at a whole range of congregations, their thinking and their activities, in different situations throughout Scotland and some of the cities of England and the United States. Hence the reference to 'the book that never was' at the start of this chapter: although much of my study leave work has fed into occasional articles that I have written and talks and workshops I have given on Iona and elsewhere, the hope and expectation was that there would be a book at the end of it. But the demands and preoccupations associated with being Leader of the Community prevented that, and because so much of what I wanted to say then was specific and contextual, and to that extent time-bound, the moment has passed.

But what I learned through these investigations and discussions on both sides of the Atlantic, on top of my own experience and the insights I have gained also through my involvement with the traditions, thinking and current concerns of the Iona Community, has helped me to develop my understanding of mission; and, while there are obvious dangers in generalising, and encouraging signs of hope and growth are certainly to be found, sometimes in surprising places, on the whole I am not enthusiastic or even very hopeful about what appear to be the priorities and the prevailing views about mission in today's churches.

The concern with church numbers is understandable, especially in a culture accustomed to measuring success and appraising value in quantifiable terms and when so many congregations are struggling both to meet their financial commitments to their local and national denominational headquarters and to maintain their buildings, the cherished heritage of a proud past but often no longer suitable to contemporary needs. But the result is a preoccupation with church growth, as if the Church and the kingdom were one and the same; and too often mission is a not very well concealed recruitment drive or, worse still, the promotion of a package. God works through the Church to be sure, and the calling of the Church to fulfil its vocation as an embodiment or foretaste of the kingdom is well-established and hard to live up to. The congregation thus has an essential role in the missionary process as channel or agent of the good news but it is not the be-all and end-all as long as the primary emphasis is on building not the Church but the kingdom, seeking to make God real to people where they are. God's purpose and promise are not limited to the Church, for God's sphere of activity is the world, of which the Church is but a part. Mission belongs to God, not to the Church; and the missionary task is thus to discern and point to the signs of the kingdom breaking through wherever this is happening, as it does both within and outside the Church, with church growth a possible and desirable by-product. Mission is about conversation rather than conversion; about engagement, interaction and dialogue rather than verbal persuasion, for the language of action and the witness of integrity and consistency carries more authenticity and credibility than slick words delivered hit-and-run style.

There are clear divisions within the churches today on issues like these which go back ultimately to different approaches to the Bible and interpretations of its authority. Is it the Bible or Jesus Christ that we stake our lives on – the words or the Word? Gerard Hughes has said, in *O God, Where Are You?*,

> The most effective policy for all true enemies of religion is the encouragement of fundamentalism in every way possible. And it is disingenuous of those who claim to hold the literal authority and verbal inspiration of the Bible in such high regard, over against those who recognise the extent to which it is conditioned by time and culture, to deny, by conveniently ignoring, for example, the internal inconsistencies and the social codes with their summary penalties, that they too are selective in their reading of it.

Mission must be focused on the world but centred on God, Jesus Christ, the Gospel and the kingdom, not on the Church; it must reach out unconditionally to proclaim the love of God without seeking to prescribe or even measure the response: 'the church's task is to help others to see what the Gospel means to them in their situation without seeking to determine in advance what the outcome will be' (J. G. Davies, *Dialogue with the World*). The American theologian Walter Wink has rightly said, in the third of his 'powers' trilogy, *Engaging the Powers*, 'In a pluralistic world in which we are privileged to learn from all religious and philosophical traditions, Christians still have a story to tell to the nations. And who knows – telling it may do no one so much good as ourselves.' An understanding of spirituality as engagement, as a dynamic, energising, open-ended process, points unequivocally and inexorably to such an approach. In a world that is hungry for meaning and purpose, for a sense of priorities and values, it does people no service to provide answers that cannot withstand rigorous scrutiny, to pretend that the Christian faith is somehow about arriving – and then everything will be all right – rather than a continuing journey of ups and downs through which God will sustain us and Jesus Christ walk with us as he accompanied the disciples on the Emmaus road.

It is according to such theological criteria and against this background that the churches' approach to mission must be appraised. Much is being made of the opportunities that the impending millennium celebrations will provide, but for the most part it would appear that the churches' plans are regrettably narrow so that the turn of the century is seen as a time for evangelisation (that is, making converts) rather than for evangelism (sharing the good news). For its part the Community will recognise the millennium appropriately through the content and focus of its islands programmes and through its support and involvement, along with both church-related and secular groups, in various campaigns relating to nuclear disarmament (Abolition 2000 and Trident Ploughshares 2000), the relief of overseas debt (Jubilee 2000) and the protection of the environment (Agenda 21).

If the Community is serious about seeking 'new ways to touch the hearts of all' we cannot avoid questions concerning approaches to mission and how we relate to the Church – or, more correctly now, the churches from which our membership is drawn. The situation has changed radically since the early days when there was a clear pioneering role in so many ways, when the Community's relationship could be straightforwardly with one particular denomination to which almost all its members belonged. Over that period the Community had an influential role within the life of the Church in the development of approaches to mission through, for instance, industrial chaplaincy, ministry in areas of urban deprivation, church centres and house groups within congregations. Now, even with the considerable impact that the Wild Goose Resource Group have had throughout the British churches, even with the occasional complimentary remarks that are made about the helpful effect the Community has in communicating its vision and integrated spirituality, the scene and social context have changed beyond recognition. Moreover, the Community while continuing to assert that it is not an alternative to the Church for those who are dissatisfied with mainstream worship and church life (and almost all Members are active in their local congregations, even if sometimes they are hanging on there only by their finger-tips) can no longer interact creatively, as happened previously, with a single denomination.

Pat Kane, pop-star with the group Hue and Cry and apostle of postmodernism *par excellence*, in one of his regular Thursday columns in *The Herald* (November 1997) discussed some of the issues raised by the rejection of a prominent woman minister as the first woman Moderator of the General Assembly of the Church of Scotland, following intense press speculation about the outcome of the election. It had been suggested that she was not elected because of alleged opposition to her on the grounds that several years previously she had 'blessed' a 'same sex union' between a lesbian couple, whereas the truth is that she is as likely not to have been elected (in a church where, despite apparent progress, gender attitudes are still a problem and deep-rooted prejudices against equal opportunities for women still prevail in many places) simply because she was a woman.

Kane went on to explore, in highly allusive fashion, what he described as the 'new lands of modern spirituality' and referred to opinion polls showing for the first time that a majority of people do not believe that God exists, suggesting, 'In this climate, surely organised Christianity needs as many new markets as possible?' What a revealing statement, with its telling reference to the market-place! He proceeded to ask 'Why can't we choose whatever religious source we want – Christian, Buddhist, Muslim, New Age – in order that we get some cosmic perspective on our limited, work-obsessed, materialistic lives?' and refers with a measure of approval to the approach of the Cambridge academic Don Cupitt, best known outside theological circles for the television *Sea of Faith* series, with his advocacy of 'a kind of post-Godly flexi-religion' – 'an experiment in self-hood' rather than involving 'a supernatural doctrine', providing spiritual tools for living through bringing rich symbols into our lives, with 'God' having to do with the embodiment of the highest human values, through a cultural rather than supernatural expression. Kane talks of a 'growing symphony of modern spiritual freedom' and interestingly sees as a major justification for spiritual exploration that 'modern Westerners need to be able to speak the language of spirituality to others, and mean it, if we do not want our global dominance to result in the most unholy wars'!

Such a jumble of ideas may seem almost impenetrable, but in the postmodern pluralist context this is typical of the challenge that has to be addressed, both at an intellectual level and in terms of the practicalities of missionary strategies and structures. There can scarcely ever have been a time when the world has been in greater need of the inspiring vision of the kingdom and the transforming message of the Gospel, that through the love and grace of God all things will be made new and a community of justice and peace, joy and harmony created. Is the Church of today and tomorrow up to it? And more particularly within the life of the Iona Community are there ways in which we can develop ideas or, better still, working 'models' that may be of assistance to the churches as they in turn reach decisions on their priorities of mission? It will be an interesting debate within the Community, not least because of the inevitable range of views to be found among Members, to the extent that some, thoroughly mistakenly I believe, feel that any discussion that focuses on the Church in this sort of way is an abandonment of our responsibility to pay attention first to the world and its needs.

One of the clear conclusions that emerged from my sabbatical studies is that there is no blueprint of an approach to mission that is transportable or universally applicable. The particular context is all-important and must be investigated, analysed and understood with a view to discerning the key features and devising an approach that is suitable both to the situation (needs-related) and to the people who are to be involved (gifts-related): there is unlikely to be much point in trying to run a youth club if all the people available as volunteers are senior citizens! I discovered many signs of encouragement, hope and growth, congregations seeking to relate imaginatively and adventurously to their local community, taking huge, courageous steps of faith without really knowing where they were going: one of the most exciting of such projects which involved both Members and Associates of the Community, in Orbiston Church at Bellshill just outside Glasgow, started with a small committed group who studied, prayed and worshipped together, developed their plans, and raised a large amount of money to start what is now a flourishing neighbourhood centre. (This story is told by Kathy Galloway in *Starting Where We Are*, published in 1998 by the Community.)

There were sharp contrasts between different settings – the city-centre church, seeking to relate to those who work and shop in its parish, will not pursue the same approach as a middle-class suburban congregation or as a church seeking to be faithful against the odds in a housing scheme where unemployment and the incidence of other social problems is high. One of the interesting phenomena of our times is the development of the church on the model of business corporation, very much a product of the ethos and values of contemporary society, one might say. Predictably perhaps this is to be found more in the United States than in Britain, although just the other day I was invited to take part in a radio discussion about such a church that had opened in London, in a converted warehouse with a capacity of thousands, high-tech amplification systems, big screens, and facilities for beaming services all over Europe and beyond, with an independent, charismatic and conservative evangelical thrust, under the leadership of an African minister who arrived in Britain a year ago with a mission to convert 'humanist Britain' to 'true Christianity'.

The examples of this approach I discovered in the United States had a different emphasis but were just as striking – the church as big business, with big staff, big programmes, and big budget. The most extreme case I visited was a flourishing congregation of thousands in the prosperous down-town area of a major city, shortly to move to shining new, purpose-built premises. The congregation included more than two-thirds of those who belonged to the denomination in the city, with the rest spread around some thirty other congregations, most inevitably struggling. But in another American city, in conversation with one of the academics I met, a very engaged and engaging nun who is an expert in liturgy, when I sought advice on where I should worship on Sunday, she suggested that I should visit not one of the big churches, which I was keen to experience for the first time, but another congregation which she described as 'crumbling' because it is in such struggling that she saw the church as truly alive and the signs of the kingdom as most evident. This was also my impression from my study leave and it is the view that the Iona Community's own experience and my thinking down the years would substantiate. God in Jesus Christ is to be encountered in a special way where there is struggle and striving for fullness of life, where there is a strong sense of pilgrimage and an openness to the Spirit: 'Blessed are the poor in spirit (or just "the poor" in Luke's version) for theirs is the kingdom of God.'

The Church's vocation in each and every locality is to be a

worshipping, healing, learning, serving community, faithfully living by the values of the kingdom, modelling and embodying a counter-cultural vision, looking and reaching out beyond itself with a wider vision, to discover the light and love of God in engagement with the life of the world, standing up and speaking out against all that diminishes and disempowers humanity. In so doing it will dream and explore; it will be open, flexible and ready to take risks; it will be generous, hospitable and ready to celebrate; it will not be a ghetto but keen to co-operate and engage; it will be a transforming community – influencing others for good, and being transformed itself in the process; it will be resilient and persistent, however hard the way and it will be marked by joy and an eagerness to celebrate.

> If the Christian community of the future is to develop spiritual resources for that struggle, resources which will strengthen and guide those who work for justice and peace in their communities and in the world, it will need to shed much of its inherited and accumulated baggage, and learn to see itself as a community of pilgrims, a community on the move. There is nothing quite like the experience of walking to promote comradeship. The Church is meant to be a people on the march, moving forward in solidarity, a pilgrim people. Sadly it often becomes a static, backward-looking people. The Church of the future has to choose between a settler mentality and a pioneer mentality. To stand still in the spiritual life is to go backwards. The pilgrim community is one which is oriented towards the future, a community marked and motivated by a divinely inspired restlessness. As the Jewish Passover was to be eaten in haste by people ready to move on, so the pilgrim community must always be moving forwards. Lot's wife looked backwards and became one of God's frozen people.
>
> A community of pilgrims who are rooted and grounded

> in Christ's resurrection will be characterised by joy. Not the bogus cheeriness of hearty, jolly, back-slapping Christians, but the deep joy of those who have attained an inner assurance, a confidence and trust in the power of the risen Christ. A pilgrim Church must be a joyful confident Church, which sings the songs of freedom in the midst of its bondage. 'Sing Alleluia and keep on walking,' says Augustine in one of his most memorable sermons. As we move into the heart of the storm we will sing but we will keep on walking. (Kenneth Leech, *The Sky is Red*)

What future does the Church have? Where does it fit in – whether to the life of the Iona Community or to the pluralist, secularised society in which we live? The debate and discussion goes on within the Community and on a much wider scale too. Some clutch at straws and think the golden days of the past can be recreated. Some see the need for change but cannot discern the way to follow. Some say the Church as it is must die for it to be reborn. But already in all sorts of ways the new Church is already emerging and in this lies the hope and the excitement.

In November 1995 in the heart of Govan, where the Community's offices are, a memorable and very moving lecture was given by a remarkable man. For over 25 years John Miller has lived with his family in one of Glasgow's housing schemes where he is the parish minister. He is widely respected and loved, not a Community Member, but close to and admired by many of us; and he spoke with the insight and authority of his experience about the missionary task facing the Church today, powerfully relating the conclusion of his address to Turner's famous painting 'The Fighting Temeraire', which he explained represents change and death:

> If I am right that the old structures have outlived their

day, that they are being tugged to their last berth to be broken up, that the church's former role will in our day be no more, if I am right about that, I am certain of this . . . It is not for its structures that the church is to be valued, but for the Word, its faith. The church is firstly and finally a matter not of structure but of the heart. And among the small incidents of a Glasgow parish of which I have spoken tonight shines an irrepressible response to life – 'like small boats, tossed by the waves, but always bobbing back' in Vaclav Havel's phrase. In this is the assurance that for the church, as for us as individuals, there surely is life beyond the breakers' yard.

O God, our mystery
we come to you, bright like a fire,
You invite us to sit with the suffering
and to seek your uncomfortable peace.
Teach us, as a Community,
to move with and through your flames;
to be inspired;
to seek new vision;
to be immersed in your creation
strong like the wind and bright like a fire.
Celebrating, weeping, changing
– alive to your extraordinary possibilities
of new life, of wholeness, of Spirit;
of friendship with Christ.
Amen

(Peter Millar, Iona, August 1998)

12

Moving Onwards

Writing this book has itself been an interesting and instructive process (and for readers who have persisted thus far I do hope that there has been a measure of interest also!). At times and to some extent (especially when the writing has taken place over a continuing period, rather than in the gaps between other preoccupations and duties during the months since the project started) it has assumed a life of its own, as other much more experienced *makars* (Scots word), particularly of novels and poetry, have themselves said in sharing insights into how their own writing is shaped. The pendulum has swung between personal memoir and more objective analysis, between specific aspects of the life and concerns of the Iona Community and the wider context, in my attempt to explore and reflect on the Community's vision and its approach to spirituality. The themes of energy, connectedness and engagement have been a constant thread, conveying a strong sense both of movement and relationship. The Iona Community has a continuing justification only if it is serving some wider purpose, doing something of value and significance, going somewhere worthwhile. So here, finally, are some thoughts on possible priorities and directions, on the tasks of today and tomorrow, on the business of 'moving on'.

One of the closing chapters in Ron Ferguson's book *Chasing the Wild Goose*, about the story of the Community, is entitled with evocative and brilliant insight, 'Dancing with a limp'. We move forward with *joie de vivre* and a spring in our step, to the accompaniment of music and laughter, but at the same time a little haltingly, recognising our frailty and vulnerability that may well cause us to stumble as the pace quickens and the manoeuvres become more complex. We have important issues to discuss, challenges to face up to, priorities to sort out.

The Community's vision and its understanding of spirituality assume even greater significance, as fixed reference points in an environment that is changing. Never, it might be said, was there greater need for those Columban gifts of courage, faith and cheerfulness, for an adventurous and resilient spirit, for a readiness to trust in God's loving purpose. We have already talked much of the external changes – the secularisation of values, the rise of individualism, all the combined effects of the technological revolution, liberalism and globalisation. Neither a theology nor a spirituality can be useful or worthwhile unless it relates to or takes account of context. A report prepared for the Council of the World Alliance of Reformed Churches held at Debrecen in Hungary in 1997 said,

> The call to witness in context challenges the witnessing church to create an inclusive community, critically engaged in action, questioning the inequality of access to resources, and recognising the positive nature of diversity in a community which is united but not uniform, and in which individuals receive from one another as well as give. Christians are personally involved in the matter of *semper reformanda*. (*Break the Chains of Injustice*)

This sums up very effectively the perspective the Community

seeks to maintain in addressing social issues, both in contributing creatively to debates and in sharing in campaigning activities, whether through the churches or as part of the culture of civil society. There are so many pressing and controversial matters that, with limited resources, it is becoming increasingly necessary to identify priorities for corporate attention, to avoid the possibility of duplication of effort, and to recognise the value both of finding ways of supporting some initiatives, in which the Community may be unable to play a full part, from a distance, and of the scope for sharing in joint alliances and coalitions on other topics.

It is clear too that in an increasingly divided world the principle of solidarity becomes ever more crucial – solidarity with one's fellow campaigners, and solidarity too with the victims of injustice and oppression. This solidarity is already expressing itself through the groundswell of resistance to the policies and values that exacerbate and create inequalities of wealth all over the world and thus thwart and undermine the possibility of flourishing that is God's purpose for all creation. The German theologian Dorothee Solle expressed this very powerfully, taking account of the spiritual significance of such developments, in the Christian Peace Conference's newsletter for January 1998, when she stressed the importance of

> communities of *solidarity* which . . . are images in miniature of another, larger, human community of solidarity, to which all human beings without exception belong . . . The 'enlightened self-interest of the individual', the intellectual basis of capitalism, leads unerringly to the increasing impoverishment of the majority of the human race and of a third of the population in the rich countries in our part of the world. It destroys all of us in the spiritual sense, when we no longer know God but only the nice idols, and when we disengage

ourselves from the human concept of solidarity in the interest of self-discovery and self-realisation.

There are stark challenges confronting us in Britain at this time, particularly in the face of world-wide economic recession, and those who may have believed that the election of a Labour government in 1997 would suddenly usher in a new era of social justice now see how mistaken they were. Indeed, writing in *The Observer* on 6 September 1998, Will Hutton explored the social consequences of the government's policies in the field of education and spoke of the creation of a self-perpetuating powerful elite and the erosion of 'public-spirited values', and came to the depressing conclusion: 'We are building one of the most unequal societies on Earth – and nobody is protesting.' Clearly there are stern challenges ahead here in the field of social policies and one of the Community's priorities will be to find the best way to share in the continuing discussions and the campaigning. And it will be particularly exciting to have the opportunity to share in the particular changes that will be taking place in Scotland with a new Parliament coming into being later in 1999 and the development of a new kind of political culture, based to some extent on the experience of the Thatcher years during which many coalitions were built and alliances forged around common interests, values and objectives.

The changing shape of the Community itself creates challenges too of an internal nature. With increasing numbers of Members and Associates, across a wide geographical spread, how do we retain our sense of belonging together? There is less intimacy and inevitably Members feel that they do not know one another as well as may have been possible previously. I still like to think of the Community as a big family, but some people are now asking, for understandable reasons, if we should wear name-badges at Community meetings. Maintaining our sense of ownership of the work done on the Community's behalf becomes more difficult as movement and organisation grow; means need to be found of ensuring that the system of accountability continues to work satisfactorily, that the sense of mutual trust is sustained and nourished, that information about what is happening or proposed is communicated swiftly and effectively.

And we are right in the middle of major exercises, which obviously cannot be handled separately, looking at the future of our mainland and our islands work. The possibility of a new mainland base is under consideration since the present accommodation is no longer adequate for our needs. We do not have enough space to house all the mainland staff together and want improved facilities for reception and welcome, for meetings, possibly for a mainland sales outlet and the development of further mainland outreach projects. The potential for debate is considerable, not least because any move is likely to require additional resources and the Community, through costly experience, is committed to 'travelling light' in relation to buildings. I can predict with confidence, however, that the discussion, heated as it may be at times, will be thorough and responsible and it will at all times not only be grounded in a strong sense of the practical realities but also informed by the shared vision and approach to spirituality.

'Have we created a monster?' asked our rediscovery of spirituality group in a paper they submitted in the consultations on the future of the Community's islands work. The question could of course be applied equally relevantly to the Community's work overall in view of the increases that have occurred over recent years in both staffing and budgets. But the issue is at its sharpest on Iona where the scale and pace have grown very significantly and all attempts to introduce and maintain a 'gentler culture' have come to naught. The model is the same as it was twenty-five years ago, it has been creaking for some time, and the pressure is no longer sustainable even although the arrangements for the support and welfare of staff have been improved. Increased numbers of guests and day visitors make increased demands on staff; and increasing the staff numbers further is not the answer, particularly in view of the limitations on space. Challenging discussions lie ahead here also, not least because there is no sign of any slackening in the demand for what the Community is offering on Iona and at Camas – the experience, through worship, work and leisure, of sharing the common life, exploring, through living it out in a sense, the incarnational theology and integrated spirituality; and we want our centres to continue to be accessible to people from a wide range of backgrounds. The feelings of Community Members run high here too: for many of them Iona represents an important part of their personal story. As for the mainland discussion we want to get it right of course, but there is a greater urgency here, both to do something to relieve the pressure and to keep the period of uncertainty as short as possible.

It is an immense privilege to be Leader of the Community at this time. I doubt whether the Community has ever stood still; but to have responsibility in relation to all these issues, not for determining the outcome but for guiding the process of discussion, is to be aware how much we are on the move at present – not because we are unsure about our purpose, our vision, our spirituality, rather because we are taking seriously our aspiration to find 'new ways to touch the hearts of all'. It is perhaps just a matter of careless planning that all these discussions should be happening at once; on the other hand this facilitates the development of a coherent approach that recognises the interconnectedness of all that we do, what might rather grandiosely be described as an integrated strategy . . . !

Through it all runs our understanding of spirituality as engagement, our trust in God's loving purpose and our sense of the inspiration and companionship of Jesus Christ. We feel we are on the move – yes, dancing with a limp with the humility that is born of our awareness of past and present shortcomings. And as our pilgrimage goes on, we maintain an openness to the future, recognising the provisionality of all our policies and decisions. Jean Vanier of L'Arche Community offers insights that are both reassuring and instructive:

> The very struggle to build community is a gift of God and in accepting it we acknowledge it as a gift, not received once and for all, but one for which we must yearn and pray and labour day after day. Since community is a living, dynamic body, it is in continual movement. It evolves as people grow, as the whole body grows in welcoming new people, as other people leave and separate to create another body, just as the cells of the body separate and multiply. Each community, as well as each person, lives its pains of growth, its times of passage.
>
> The danger for all of us is to want a community that is strong and competent with the security of wealth, good administration and structures, and experienced, competent, committed people. None of us like to live in insecurity, in fear of tomorrow. We are all like Peter, afraid of walking on the waters. So we can quickly close our hearts, forgetting the call of Jesus and how he brought us to life through his guiding hand. (*The Broken Body*)

Over the last few months of his time on Iona, before handing over to Brian Woodcock as Warden at the end of August 1998, Peter Millar, in a series of sermons and reports, as he prepared to move on himself, shared his own views on the future of the Community's work, on Iona in particular but on the mainland too. In his final report to the Islands Committee, he drew attention to the work of the influential American lay theologian, William Stringfellow and traced the strong similarity between some of the key features of Stringfellow's thinking and the Community's own concerns. He referred to Stringfellow's rootedness in Scripture, his close proximity to the marginalised, his sense of outrage at oppression, and his stress on four characteristics of Christian social ethics – realism about the world and understanding of contemporary culture, the recovery of passion ('the energy derived from yearning' in Kenneth Leech's phrase), radicalism rooted in prayer, and intercession and care for the poorest. Peter went on to say:

> These various threads, articulated and expressed in many dimensions, have been securely woven into the Iona Community's history. I believe that they continue to permeate the work on the islands. Their maintenance can only be rooted in imaginative prayer, the acceptance of mystery at the heart of human experience, the ongoing rediscovery of our intuitive understanding, and the recognition of our interconnectedness with creation and our suffering world. It is a moment of great learning for the whole of the Iona Community as it seeks to discover new and uncharted dimensions of its ministry. It is also a moment of incredible opportunity and challenge. In such a situation who could not be energised and hopeful? . . . Whatever direction our future work takes (both on the mainland, and on the islands) it will remain true to Christ if, at its heart, it moves with 'a strong sense of the provisional'. That means many things – incompleteness, inconsistency, exploration, radicalism, prophecy, risk-taking, the gentle acceptance of failure, the excitement of visionary plans, and also an incredibly deep affirmation from countless women and men around the globe . . . We stand, as a global community, at a place of enormous possibility and also of overwhelming threat. In it all, our islands work is a tiny fragment in the multiple purposes of God. But what is so important is that it *is* a fragment and in its own particular way is recovering social holiness and a recognition that the fate of the soul is the fate of our social order. It is certainly not a time for the Community to be discouraged: we are more needed than ever!

This is a very fine summary of all that I too have been trying to say about the vision and spirituality of the Community through the preceding pages. It is an interesting and very moving reflection of how two rather different people (as most who know us both would agree!) can have such consistency of views on matters of deep importance to them.

And so the Community's pilgrimage goes on. For all those of us who belong to it its vision will continue to inspire us, our fellow Members will continue without doubt to challenge and support us, and its approach to spirituality will underpin us through the vagaries and vicissitudes of our own lives. As we move on in our exploration, in our search for wholeness and fullness, our questioning will continue too – healthy questions about the direction and priorities of the Community, and questions also about the whys, wheres, hows, and whats of our own lives.

Malcolm Brown, Director of the William Temple Foundation, in his 1997 Second Andrewtide Lecture, delivered at St Andrews Church, Bedford, referred to Bishop Peter Selby's book *Grace and Mortgage*, where he examines Dietrich Bonhoeffer's penetrating question, 'Who is Jesus Christ for us today?' and goes on to say that 'if we are to find answers to that question we cannot retreat from the world but must maintain an engagement with the political life around us . . . And to do so we must ask three questions: who am I (the question of identity), who we are (the question of solidarity) and whose tomorrow is it to be (the question of discernment).' Here yet again we see the strands that have threaded through this book intertwining – in what have been called (by Professor Mary Grey, while leading a week on Iona in the summer of 1998, and developing a thought of Thomas Merton) 'epiphanies of interconnectedness'. This is the essence of spirituality, the energy and engagement, so that it is 'expressed not just in particular devotional acts but in a whole way of life oriented to the living God, who becomes our constant point of reference and our decisive, focal point of value' (Thomas F. Best, in a preparatory paper approaching the theme of the Eighth Assembly of the WCC – 'Turn to God; Rejoice in Hope!').

While through this book I have been reflecting in particular on the Iona Community's understanding of spirituality, which is evident in the way we pursue our concerns and carry out our activities, I hope it has been very clear that we do not lay any exclusive claim to an approach that emphasises such themes as engagement, integration, and energy. Far from it: we are continually encouraged by the discovery of groups and individuals with whom we can make common cause, who have similar priorities in relation to the proclamation of the Gospel and the values of the kingdom. To that extent I hope that this particular exploration should not be regarded as too distinctive to the Iona Community but may be perceived as having a general relevance, helpful to others on their own journey. However high-flown our hopes and aspirations, we have to get out of bed and brush our teeth each morning. God's promises and purposes embrace all time and space but were revealed conclusively and very specifically in historical events. God's energy touches our lives in ways that are thoroughly down-to-earth.

So I can think of no better way to conclude than with a reflective poem which had its inspiration in a particular time and place and really encapsulates and catches the spirit of everything I have tried to say. It is appropriate that it should refer to and have been written at Camas during the New Members' work week in July 1998 – because at Camas, with its closeness to nature and the open, honest relationships it encourages, there are ways in which the idea of spirituality comes specially alive and through the New Members programme these themes of energy and engagement are particularly experienced. The poem was written by Neil Squires, a social worker and ceilidh fiddler from Glasgow, who was hallowed into full membership of the Community during Community Week 1998.

Camas Reflection

Give me some more of these silences
The kind that are filled with the sounds of creation
Like the constant ebb and flow of the sea
Or directionless noise of wind and rain
Or the solitary cry of an oyster catcher, echoing
against granite.

Give me some more of these silences
The kind that just hang in timeless security
Enabling my mind to drift into uncharted places
So comforting, so reassuring – the moment never
needs to end.

Give me some more of these conversations
Like the ones I've had along the track,
by the sink, in the garden, round the fire,
building boxes, sewing tents, painting signs,
digging earth.

Give me some more of these conversations
The kind that help gain understanding,
break down barriers, challenge assumptions
The kind that inspire me to move beyond
conversation, into action.

Give me some more of this friendship
The kind that allows me to be vulnerable
Valued, accepted for who I am
Away from familiar constraints and expectations –
where an idea is quashed, or maybe goes unnoticed.

Give me some more of this friendship
The kind where a hug is never far off

And tea for twenty is never much hassle
Where there's plenty of music and singing and
laughter
Yet where raw edges can't be ignored.

Give me some more of this simple lifestyle
When wholesome food, heart pumping exercise
and pure, clean air just makes so much sense.

Give me some more of this simple lifestyle
Where absence of so-called comforts
Like electricity, hot water and flush toilets,
don't really matter
Where all our rushing around, work deadlines,
heavy meetings and stressful phonecalls,
seem so unimportant.

This simple lifestyle frees the mind, lifts the spirit,
gives space to think, relaxes my body, feeds my
creativity,
gives life a new perspective.

Give me some more of this life together
Where, in this special place
So small, so secluded
Yet so connected to the world
We find a spiritual meaning in the rhythms of
our day.

Give me some more of this life together
Where the depth of our relationships
Is carried in our hearts
And our experience goes beyond this place
To inspire and challenge us
And fill us with hope.

At Columba's bay
they met;
two of Iona's pilgrims.
He a pastor from Zaire;
She a broker from Detroit.
And battered by the
autumn wind and rain
they shared their stories.
Twentieth-century stories –
rooted in contrasting realities,
yet both embedded
in a strange, life-giving
brokenness.
The hidden stories –
of poverty and torture,
of cancer and loneliness;
interweaving stories,
mirroring our
global interconnectedness.
And stories of faith;
of God's unfolding
in their lives
through ordinary days.
And suddenly
it seemed
that for a moment
on that distant shore
they glimpsed
that basic truth –
that truly,
we are one
in Christ.

(Peter Millar, *An Iona Prayer Book*)

God of all creation –
who cannot be contained by our boundaries
or our definitions –
light from beyond the galaxies,
sea without a farther shore.
You are present in every distinct place,
In every moment in history.
You are here and now.
Help us to understand
That those from whom we are separated in life
By distance, by sea and land;
Those from whom we are separated
By difference, by prejudice,
By language, by lack of communication;
And those from whom we are separated in death,
By its long silence, its aching absence –
Are each of them in your presence:
That beyond our horizons,
Beyond our boundaries
Beyond our understanding,
They are in your embrace. Amen
(Jan Sutch Pickard, *Vice Versa*)

Selected Bibliography

Bakare, Sebastian, *The Drumbeat of Life* (World Council of Churches, 1997).

Bell, John, *States of Bliss and Yearning: The Marks and Means of Authentic Christian Spirituality* (Wild Goose Publications, 1998).

Bradley, Ian, *The Celtic Way* (Darton, Longman and Todd, 1995)

Bradley, Ian, *Columba, Pilgrim and Penitent* (Wild Goose Publications, 1996)

Brueggemann, Walter *The Prophetic Imagination* (SCM,1978)

Capra, Fritjof, *The Turning Point* (Flamingo, 1982).

Church of Scotland Panel on Worship, *Pray Now* (St Andrew Press, 1998).

Clancy, Thomas Owen, and Gilbert Márkus, *Iona – the Earliest Poetry of a Celtic Monastery* (Edinburgh, University Press, 1995).

Craig, Maxwell (ed.), *For God's Sake – Unity* (Wild Goose Publications, 1998).

Davies, J. G., *Dialogue with the World* (SCM Press, 1967).

Dorr, Donal, *Integral Spirituality* (Gill and Macmillan, 1990).

Ferguson, Ron *George MacLeod* (Collins, 1990).

Ferguson, Ron, *Chasing the Wild Goose* (revised edn, Wild Goose Publications,1998)
Fraser, Ian, *Living a Countersign* (Wild Goose Publications, 1990).
Fraser, Ian, *Strange Fire* (Wild Goose Publications, 1994).
Gibbs, Mark and T. Ralph Morton, *God's Frozen People* (Fontana, 1964).
Gibbs, Mark and T. Ralph Morton, *God's Lively People* (Fontana, 1971).
Galloway, Kathy (ed.), *The Pattern of Our Days* (Wild Goose Publications, 1996).
Galloway, Kathy, *Starting Where We Are* (Wild Goose Publications, 1998).
Hope, Stanley, *A Very British Monster* (Wild Goose Publications, 1997).
Hughes, Gerard, *God of Surprises* (Darton, Longman and Todd, 1985).
Hughes, Gerard, *God, Where Are You?* (Darton, Longman and Todd, 1997).
Iona Community, *The Wee Worship Book* (Wild Goose Publications, 1989).
Iona Community, *What is the Iona Community?* (revised edn, Wild Goose Publications, 1996).
The Iona Community Worship Book (Wild Goose Publications, 1990).
Leech, Kenneth, *The Eye of the Storm* (Darton, Longman and Todd, 1992).
Leech, Kenneth, *The Sky is Red* (Darton, Longman and Todd, 1997).
Lodge, David, *Therapy* (Penguin, 1995).
MacArthur, Mairi, *Columba's Isle* (Iona Press, 1995).
MacArthur, Mairi, *Iona* (Colin Baxter, 1997).
MacIntyre, Alasdair, *After Virtue* (Duckworth, 1981).
MacIntyre, Alasdair, *Whose Justice, Which Rationality?* (Duckworth, 1988).

Merton, Thomas, *Thoughts in Solitude* (Burns and Oates, 1958).
Merton, Thomas, *Contemplative Prayer* (Darton, Longman and Todd, 1973).
Millar, Peter, *An Iona Prayer Book* (Canterbury Press, 1998).
Morton, Ralph, *The Iona Community: Personal Impressions of the Early Years* (St Andrew Press, 1970).
Nouwen, Henri, *Reaching Out* (Fount, 1979).
Pickard, Jan Sutch, *Vice Versa* (Church in the Market Place Publications, 1997).
Puls, Joan and Gwen Cashmore, *Soundings in Spirituality* (The Ecumerical Spirituality Project, 1996).
Ritchie, Anna, *Iona* (Batsford, 1997).
Sacks, Jonathan, *The Persistence of Faith* (Weidenfeld and Nicholson, 1991).
Selby, Peter, *Grace and Mortgage* (Darton, Longman and Todd, 1997).
Social Affairs Unit, *Faking It: The Sentimentalism of Modern Society* (1998).
Vanier, Jean, *Community and Growth* (Darton, Longman and Todd, 1979).
Vanier, Jean, *The Broken Body* (Darton, Longman and Todd, 1988).
de Waal, Esther, *A World Made Whole* (Fount, 1991).
Wild Goose Resource Group, *Cloth for the Cradle* (Wild Goose Publications, 1997).
Wink, Walter, *Engaging the Powers* (Fortress,1992).
World Alliance of Reformed Churches, *Breaking the Chains of Injustice* (WARC, 1997).
World Council of Churches, *A Christian Spirituality for Our Times* (WCC, 1994).

Histories of Iona: *Columba's Isle* and *Iona* by Mairi MacArthur – herself from an Iona family – are highly accessible and informative; for a more specialist work, relating particularly to the archaeological aspects, Anna Ritchie's *Iona* is recommended.

The Iona Community has its own publishing department producing a range of books, tapes, CDs and liturgical resources relating to the concerns of the Community. Enquiries to and catalogues from Wild Goose Publications, Unit 15, 8 Harmony Row, Glasgow G51 3BA; telephone: 0141-440-0985.

If you are interested in finding out more . . .

- Any detailed questions about the work and concerns of the Iona Community, including information about how to become an Associate Member or Friend of the Community, should be addressed to the Iona Community, Pearce Institute, 840 Govan Road, Glasgow, G51 3UU.

- Enquiries about staying at Iona Abbey, the MacLeod Centre or Camas should be addressed to the Bookings Secretary, Iona Abbey, Isle of Iona, Argyll, PA76 6SN.

- Information about opportunities for working on Iona or at Camas, as a member of the resident staff or a volunteer, can be obtained from the Staff Co-ordinator, Iona Abbey, Isle of Iona, Argyll, PA76 6SN.